PICTURES IN PATCHWORK

...

A Fresh Look at Tradition

PICTURES IN PATCHWORK

A Fresh Look at Tradition

Laurie Swim

BLANDFORD

A BLANDFORD BOOK
First published in the UK 1991
by Blandford
(a Cassell imprint)
Villiers House
41/47 Strand
LONDON
WC2N 5JE

First published in the United States as *Quilting*

PICTURES IN PATCHWORK
was prepared and produced by
Michael Friedman Publishing Group, Inc.
15 West 26th Street
New York, New York 10010

Editor: Sharyn Rosart
Art Director: Jeff Batzli
Designer: Lynne Yeamans
Photography Editor: Ede Rothaus
Illustrator: Steven Arcella

Typeset by The Interface Group, Inc.
Printed and bound in Hong Kong by Leefung-Asco Printers Ltd.

British Library Cataloguing in Publication Data
Swim, Laurie
Pictures in patchwork.
1. Patchwork
I. Title
746.46

ISBN 0-7137-2308-4

ACKNOWLEDGMENTS

Thank you, Ann Bird and Doris Waddell,
for so generously sharing your knowledge with me.

DEDICATION

To Larry and our son Jacob

CONTENTS

Aedh Wishes for the Cloths of Heaven

Had I the heaven's embroider'd cloths,
Enwrought with golden and silver light,
The blue and the dim and the dark cloths
Of night and light and the half light
I would spread the cloths under your feet:
But I, being poor, have only my dreams;
I have spread my dreams under your feet;
Tread softly because you tread on my dreams.

—William Butler Yeats

Opposite page: **Four Seasons,** *by Anne de la Mauviniere Silva*

Today's Themes, Tomorrow's Traditions

The tradition of quilting in North America has continued from pioneer times, having survived most strongly in rural communities until the Sixties. At that time, with the revival of interest in traditional roots and the rise of the women's movement, quilting came to be more popular and, over the last twenty years, has come to be accepted as an art form.

Diversification from traditional patterns came when quilters began to explore the unlimited possibilities in design themes, choice of color, fabric, and form. We have long passed the time when we only repeat the designs found in traditional patterns. What has remained, and what connects us to our past, are the aesthetic and social aspects of the medium.

Fabric manufacturers have become more attentive to the needs of quilters. Prints are widely available, and the quilters are paying more attention to types of fabric. Natural fibers, such as one hundred percent cotton, have found a new audience in quilters—these are more manageable as small pieces in appliqué and piecing methods, whether machine-sewed or done by hand. They are softer and more malleable than synthetic fiber blends. Other types of fabrics have been used experimentally, mostly for contrasting texture and achieving different effects. Quilting has become an individual form of expression; shared knowledge, tools and materials are readily available to just about anyone who is interested.

Marcel Duchamp's
Nude Descending a Staircase.

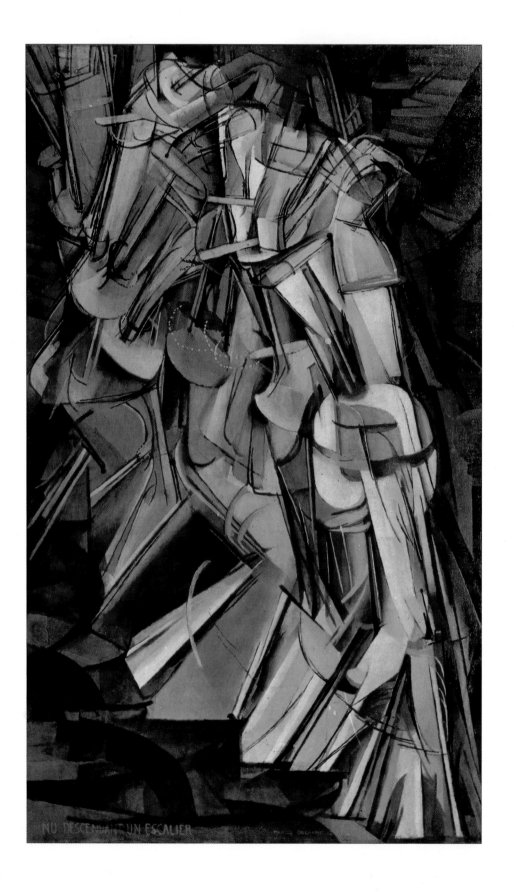

Quilters generally agree that it is best to begin by studying the traditional designs and methods before breaking out on your own. A solid background of technical knowledge will take you through the rough spots. Innovative solutions will help you work out some of the tougher problems.

For both design strength and peace of mind, simplicity is the best approach. Complicated designs often end up as busywork and fail. Intricacy does not automatically equal beauty. A balance must be struck in finding the right amount of each element of your proposed piece.

Nude Descending a Staircase, *a famous abstract cubist painting by Marcel Duchamp, (now there's an idea for a quilt!) balances the breakup of form and space. That is what you should first try to achieve in your quiltwork using color, form, and texture, whether your work is figurative or geometric. No single element should dominate the work. Theme integrated with technical skill is the surest route to success. The process will enhance your design.*

Finding that balance is the thrust of this book. My purpose in writing this book is to take away your inhibitions as you strive to create your own designs and realize them in your finished work. I want to put you in charge of the medium. I want you to be able to draw upon the past, and yet not be limited by it. I want you to develop your skills to the point where you are in control of the outcome.

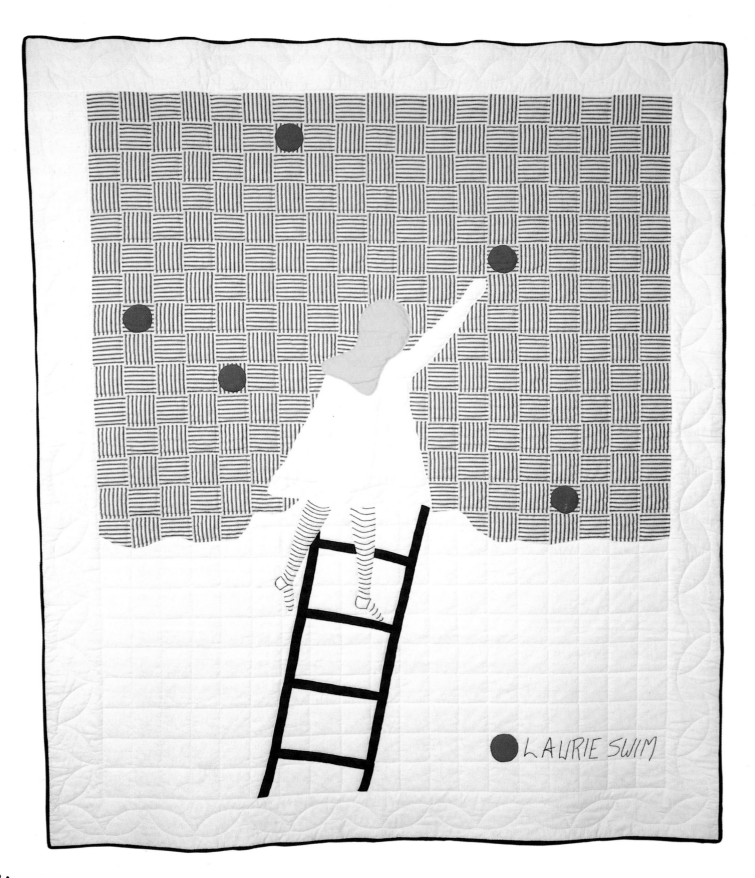

Begin the process with an image or impression, then look for the technique and fabric best suited to express that idea. Record what inspires you, with words and sketches. These will naturally reflect the times of your life. You will draw upon them over time as your inspiration, and they will become your themes. These will become tomorrow's traditions. This approach will give you unlimited possibilities with which to begin working.

As you develop your idea, you narrow the possibilities, refining the choices of techniques and fabrics. The world is your palette, to begin with. As you define the form your work is to take, you set your own boundaries, not the other way around.

Let me give you an example. I always refer to Eve's Apple *as my apprenticeship quilt. What I learned from this piece stays with me to this day.*

In a juried competition, it was awarded first prize. It was conceived in 1974 as a card design while I was living in Denmark, apprenticed to a weaver. The Danish influence is apparent in the design. It is simple: Stark black and white with two primary color accents.

Here are some of the reason for its success. This work was made in bed-quilt format, and its construction techniques combined piecing, appliqué, reverse appliqué, with some elements of the whole-cloth quilt. It covers a lot of ground for one quilt, yet it is a minimalist design so each part has to be strong enough to support the structure of the whole.

The image, to begin with, was a picture of a girl picking apples out of a tree. Once I had decided on my color scheme, my attention turned to interpreting the foliage. Since I was studying weaving at the time, it occurred to me to borrow the weaving pattern known as the log cabin. This pattern not only filled in the tree appropriately, but coincidentally echoed the rungs of the ladder. Other elements fell into place, such as using the positive form of the girl as a negative shape cut from the assembled foliage fabric.

The need for accents of color seemed a natural progression, as were the embroidered stockings and signature. All this took place in the drawing before I considered it as a quilt design. The repeated square in the tree is what finally triggered the idea of it becoming a quilt. From there the finished quilt flowed.

The large area of white was quilted in a grid, reflecting the pieced squares, which were made of mattress ticking. The leafy border was repeated in the border of Eve's skirt. Finally, and what really lifts the piece out of the ordinary, is the sense of yearning in the girl's gesture as she reaches beyond her grasp. The piece expands the idea of the Robert Browning poem that states "A man's reach must exceed his grasp" to include women. This single subtle gesture is the philosophical element that makes Eve's Apple *a work of substance.*

In the pages that follow, study the works of your fellow quilters for the imagery, balance and design, discipline of technique, and the richness of spirit that imbues them. Strive to achieve these in your own work. This endeavor will enrich you and those around you, whatever the result.

CHAPTER ONE

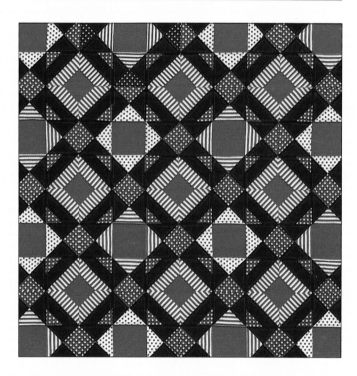

Stepping Past Tradition:
Pieced and Patchwork Quilts

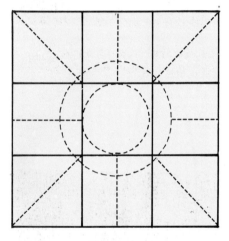

The quilting pattern of this nine-patch visually changes the finished block.

Necessity being the mother of invention, limitation of available goods and services in the New World in the seventeenth and eighteenth centuries seems to have provided a very good incentive for the development of innovative ideas. If a required item is not readily available, it is human nature to strive to create from what can be found at hand to do the job. If this innovation works, the creator goes on to refine the design, often aesthetically as well as functionally.

In the pioneering days of North America, when the patchwork quilt flourished, all materials were in limited supply. The pieced quilt might have originated out of necessity, but artistry soon evolved, for it is a basic human desire to be creative.

I recently discovered a nine-patch quilt exemplifying this process on a bed in a museum. The nine-patch is one of the simplest quilt block patterns in existence. It consists of three squares across by three squares down, forming a block. In this particular block, the center squares are all one particular color, which forms a cross. The corner squares, which complete the block, are all of another color.

Usually the quilting conforms to the outline of each square in the block, but in this case the creator quilted a circle within the center square, then another circle touching the corners of the center square. Each corner square was quilted diagonally. Quilting divided each of the remaining squares in half.

This simple quilting variation gives the block a whole new dimension. You actually have to look twice to see it as just a simple nine-patch. It is this kind of creative twist that makes pieced quilts endlessly fascinating.

I've found several examples of contemporary quilt makers who have not only given us a fresh look at tradition, but renewed our interest as we appreciate what went into the original patterns. The delight of the creator, on discovering what could be done with bits of color and geometric patterning, is evident. I'd like to take you down that path of discovery.

A simple pattern, perhaps the simplest of all in concept, is the one-patch quilt, which uses a repeated single shape to great effect. Here it is used like a pointillist painting. *Pearson Charm,* by Ann Bird, uses the square one-patch to create a landscape of mountains and their reflection. Some squares are made up of two fabrics. *Aphrodite,* by Jocelyn Patenaude, uses the hexagonal one-patch to depict a nude in a bathtub.

Right: The hexagon one-patch depicts a nude in a bathtub in Aphrodite, by Jocelyn Patenaude. Below: Like a pointillist painting, the one-patch creates a landscape in Pearson Charm, by Ann Bird.

Laurrie Sobie subtly uses the nine-patch block in Pat's Pergola Dreams.

Gloria, by John Willard, uses the traditional nine-patch as one of the elements in the design of this contemporary quilt.

Above: Recutting and reassembling in strip-piecing produces the natural rambling of leaves in the trees of **Guardians,** *by Erika Carter.*
Right: In **Black and White Study with Apple,** *Ralph Beney shows how effective contrasting strip-piecing can be.*

I remember going through an exercise in a painting class in which we had to break up a scene into many small blocks of color. Viewed from a distance, the image comes back into focus. That's what these quilts do with simple shapes in fabric.

Strip-piecing is a machine-sewing method used for creating exciting, quick, and satisfying patchwork. It is another term for the technique of piecing used by the Seminole Indians. To begin with, fabric strips of different colors are sewn together to form a new surface. These can be recut and reassembled in as many variations as the imagination allows. *Black and White Study with Apple* is a straightforward example of this technique. Equally impressive is *Guardians* for its rendering of trees in strip-piecing.

String-quilting is often used in combination with strip-piecing, as in the lyrical *Canadian Suite.* Each strip is machine-sewn to a layer of batting and backing as the piece is assembled.

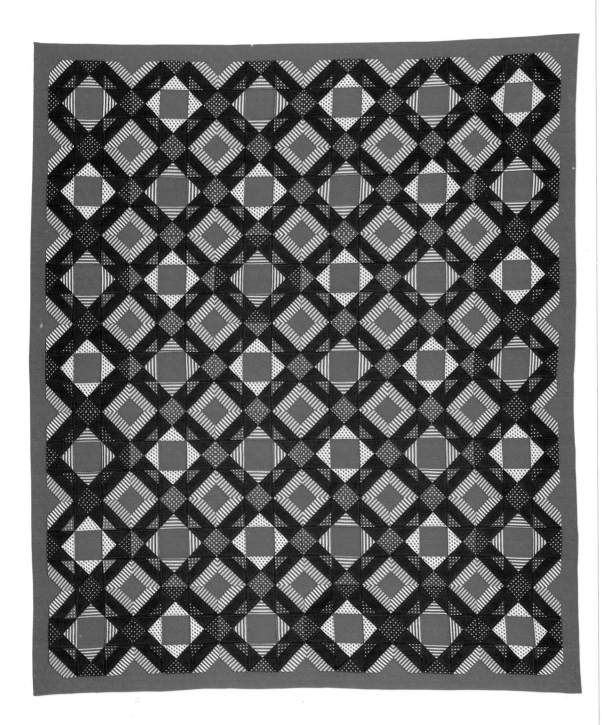

Left: **Jackknife Block,** *by Marg Caza, shows how effective a repeat block can be in simple geometric shapes and contrasting fabrics. Above: String quilting is often combined with strip-piecing as in* **Canadian Suite,** *by Ann Bird.*

In the work *Reflections and Illusions III,* curved strips of fabric have been used to create the wave effect in the center section of the quilt. This has been achieved through piecing, not appliqué, and is combined with straight-edge piecing. The central square with the circle appears to float, enhancing the beauty and symmetry of the geometric design very effectively.

The bare bones of this method of piecing is to cut multiple layers of different colors of stacked fabric. Reassembling them in the same cutting order, but in a different color sequence, creates a variety of visual combinations. Marilyn Stothers, who developed this new technique, explains it more completely in her book, *Curved Strip Piecing—A New Technique.* The possibilities of this technique shed a whole new light in the area of strip-piecing.

The quilt block is what we traditionally think of when we recall the quilts made by our grandmothers. Each block is usually made up of geometric shapes pieced together. The blocks are assembled and sewn together as a quilt top. Batting and backing are added, and then it is quilted. A more recent development is to complete each block separately, including the quilting, and to then assemble them into a larger work. Block construction can be as simple and lovely as *Flower Garden,* by Sheila Brokloff.

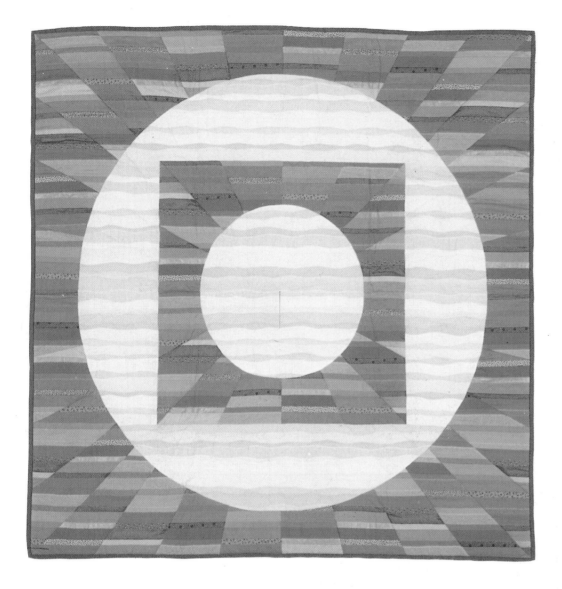

Inside the circular areas of **Reflections and Illusions III**, Marilyn Stothers uses her own technique of curved strip-piecing, in contrast with the straight strip-pieced areas of the squares. The simple round and square shapes float and radiate at the same time.

Opposite page: **Flower Garden** *is a friendship quilt. Nine-patch blocks were exchanged among the Thousand Islands Quilters Guild. Sheila Brokloff is a member. In assembling her quilt she took apart some of the blocks to integrate them into the border, using all that was given her.* **Flower Garden** *is Sheila's first quilt.*

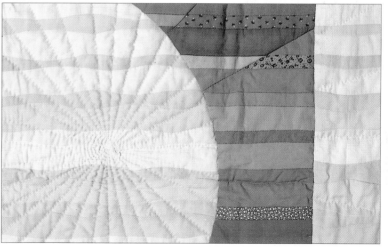

Right: A Victorian log cabin quilt from the Museum of American Folk Art. Below right: **Morning Graze,** *by Flavin Glover, shows a unique treatment of the traditional log cabin pattern. Below left: Detail of how the sheep are made.*

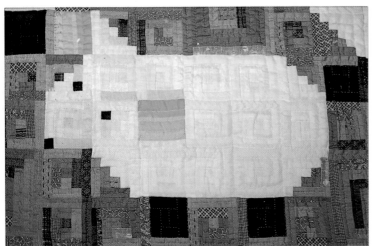

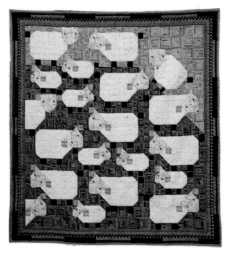

Let's take a look at the log cabin quilt block, a perennial favorite. The log cabin pattern with its traditional red center square, representing the hearth fire, and simple strips built out concentrically, has been explored continuously. Another variation is the courthouse steps pattern. It even thrived in Victorian times, when silks, satins, and velvets were the rage and mostly used for crazy quilts. Because of the precious nature of the fabrics, the end results were decorative throws, coverings for tables, and drapes for windows in the parlor.

The log cabin was one of the few pieced patterns that continued in use during this period. The strength of this pattern is still being explored today. Quilters continue to surprise us by coming up with endless variety. Note how the sheep are made up in *Morning Graze*, by Flavin Glover. Color and depth are explored in the log cabin pattern used by Anne de la Mauviniere Silva in *Fall*.

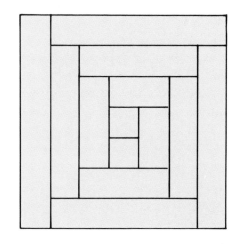

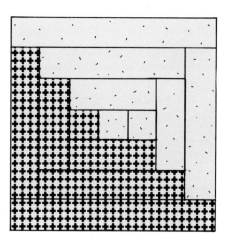

The log cabin is made up of strips built out concentrically.

Left: Anne de la Mauviniere Silva displays spontaneity of colour and texture in her use of the log cabin pattern in **Fall.**

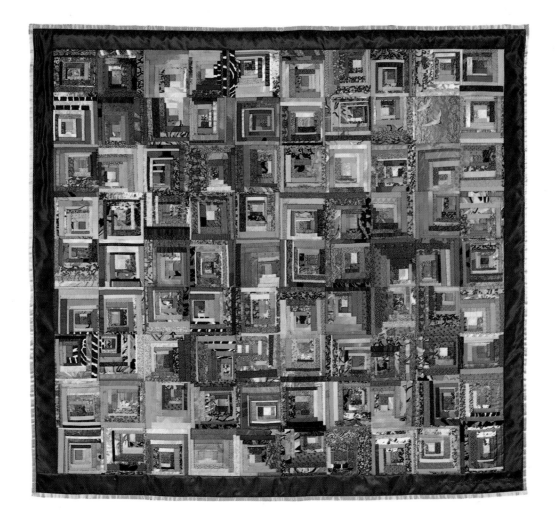

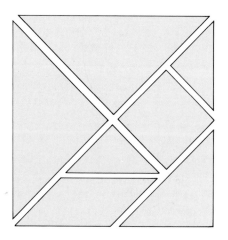

The Tangram, *a Chinese puzzle.*

Below right: **Tangram Aerobics** *shows some of the figures made up from the puzzle, which were appliquéd into a wall-hanging by Jackie Van Fossen.*

This brings us to designing our own pieced quilt block. I have decided to use a Chinese puzzle called a tangram as the starting point. A tangram is comprised of one square subdivided into seven geometric shapes. These shapes are a parallelagram, a square, and five triangles of three different sizes. The challenge of the puzzle is to arrange these shapes into different figures, of which there are hundreds of variations. I have picked out a few for you to try here. You can find books of tangrams at your local library or bookstore if you are interested in pursuing this as an avenue of design. You can also develop your own combinations.

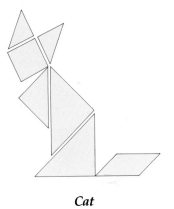

Cat

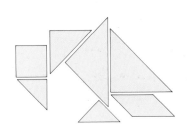

Crow

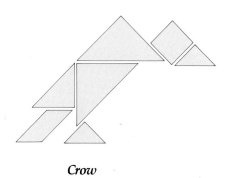

Crow

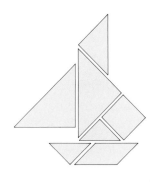

Sailboat

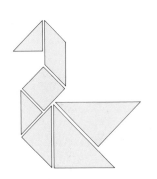

Rooster

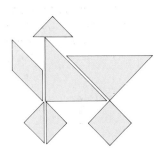

Swan

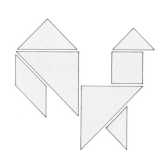

Baby Carriage

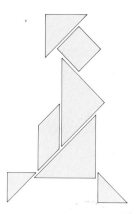

Walking Figure

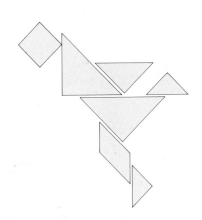

Skating Figure

Strolling Figure

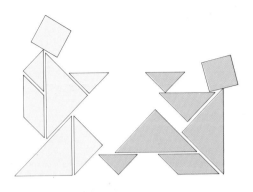

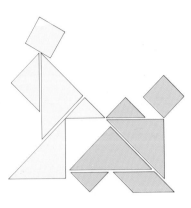

Two Tangram figures and the beginning of their integration.

Eliminating some of the shapes simplifies the figures.

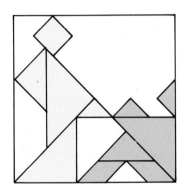

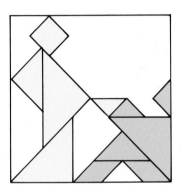

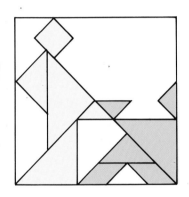

The figures are modified to fit directly within the square.

The switching of one triangle where the hands of the figures touch creates the image of a bowl being exchanged.

Dividing the block into four equal triangles allows easier piecing in four sections.

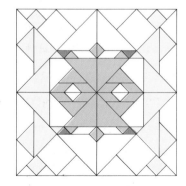

To create this four block arrangement, the original block is reversed for a second block. Blocks three and four are mirror images of the top two.

As a sample block I have chosen two figures—one sitting, one standing—and combined them within the confines of a square. I then cut up two 6-inch (15-cm) squares into tangrams, each on a different colored piece of construction paper. On a sheet of white paper I drew a 12-inch (30-cm) square to represent my quilt block and assembled my figures within this format. Having done this, I started eliminating some of the shapes so the figures better relate to each other. This became my model.

In order to work the pattern more simply into a quilt block, I then drew a 3-inch (7.5-cm) square on a piece of paper and

of the handmade object.)

At this time I realized I could divide my block format into four equal triangles by drawing diagonal lines from each corner. This would allow me to piece the different shapes in four sections when I came to assemble the fabric.

Within the borders of these four triangles, I extended straight lines from the existing geometric shapes. This resulted in new geometric shapes outside the main figures for the block's background.

Now, just for fun, compare the original tangrams to my final block. Through modification I have eliminated and rearranged some of the shapes found in the original figures but maintained their character just the same.

In keeping with the old-fashioned nomenclature of pieced blocks, I have named mine *Angel of Mercy*, because I see the standing figure as an angel ministering to the sitting figure—a homeless person. Further to the design of the whole quilt, the block can be flopped and pieced together to complete the head shape of the sitting figure when it is placed next to the first block. By turning these two blocks upside down and joining them to the bottom of the first two we begin to see an overall pattern emerge. Thus a new quilt block pattern has been born.

using a small, clear plastic, right-angled triangle from a geometry set, I redrew the figures, this time modifying the shapes so that they fit directly within the borders of the square.

I then redrew the silhouette of each figure in a series of 3-inch (7.5-cm) squares. For effect, in just a few areas of the quilt I have switched the small triangles where the hands of the figures meet, as if the standing figure is giving the seated figure a bowl of food. (I have sometimes spotted in a quilt a patterned piece eccentrically placed. Whether through lapse or at the whim of the piecer, this kind of personal touch adds to the charm

A Gallery of Pieced and Patchwork Quilts

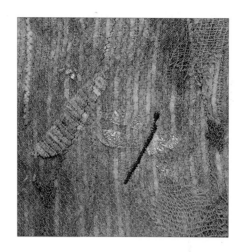

*I designed **Manitoba Afternoon**
(14 feet by 40 inches or 4 by 1 m), to fit
into a corner of a lobby. The field was
created by different shapes and colors
of netting as well as scraps of fabric
trapped under a top layer of netting
and machine-stitched.*

Judith Passing *measures 50 by 40 inches (125 by 100 cm). To create the feeling of distance, I used an underlay as well as an overlay of dark pink organza at the horizon line. For the finer branches in the foreground, yarn was randomly knotted and coached. The whole piece is mounted on soft polyurethane foam.*

Vicki Johnson's **A Bright Winter Day in Mendocino**, *measures 65 by 82 inches (162 by 205 cm). This much-celebrated quilt flows between two mediums, thus integrating piecing with painting. This is done so well you have to look twice to see where one ends and the other begins.*

Summer Serenity, *by Barbara Schaeffer, combines appliqué and piece-work successfully and seemingly without effort. The central area of water is strip-pieced; the quilting gives it fluidity. The appliqué figures of the Amish family give the work a focus.*

Kaleidoscopic Galaxy, *80 by 108 inches (200 by 270 cm), by Nancy Wikant, is a hexagonal one-patch with lovely darks and lights of patterned and solid fabrics. It makes one think of the sunlight breaking through trees or the reflection in a pool of water.*

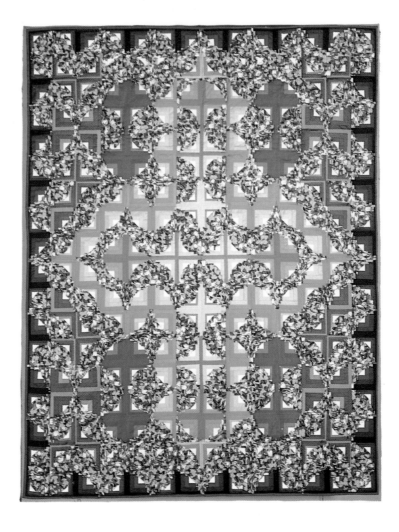

*Left: An intriguing black and white piece, **Pianissimo** (64 by 64 inches or 160 by 160 cm), by Anne de la Mauviniere Silva, uses the traditional log-cabin pattern as its point of departure. Right: **Humauresque**, by Anne de la Mauviniere Silva, is based on the log cabin pattern. It bears a close relationship to a view through a marble-headed kaleidoscope.*

Left: **Autumn,** *by Judith Tinkl, is a disciplined color play made up of small triangles in the central area and larger and larger ones as it reaches the border, giving it a sense of growth.*
Right: **Chimney Close,** *by Sylvia Price (80 by 100 inches or 200 by 250 cm) is a variation on the traditional school house block, creating new interest in an old pattern by combining piecing with appliqué.*

CHAPTER TWO

Designing an Original
Appliqué Quilt

I have viewed a lot of pictorial appliqué that has been created with much well-meaning effort but ultimately has been unsuccessful because the design is weak. Often the problem could have been resolved before the needle entered the fabric. My sympathy goes to the person brave enough to try something original only to have it fall short of expectations. When it has happened to me, my consolation has been that I'll try to do better next time. At the same time, I have chastised myself for not being more strict at the planning stage of the design.

This chapter presents different approaches for refining your designs. I hope to take away some of the mystery surrounding creating on your own. For those interested in designing for pictorial appliqué, these methods should improve your skills.

In discussions about learning to draw, the point has been made that no one expects to pick up a violin and be able to play a tune. Why then would one expect to pick up a pencil and draw perfectly well? In my lifetime I have known many people who draw, not a few of whom make their living at it. Yet, I have met only two who have the innate ability to draw effortlessly and from memory, without models.

According to Betty Edwards, author of *Drawing on the Right Side of the Brain,* we must learn to use the right hemisphere of the brain in order to draw what we see. The left side— which governs verbal, logical, and linear thought patterns—is what we were encouraged to develop in school. The right side—being nonverbal, intuitive, and spatial—was not thought of as important.

It is an interesting concept to explore and you might like to read the book. I've modified some of the exercises from that book and tailored them to direct you in designing for your own fabric originals. After reading and attempting several approaches presented here, you are invited to innovate on your own.

Opposite page: Balancing choice of accents in fabric with textural stitchery is a challenge in a fabric wall-hanging. Rose di Zio combines the qualities of the fabric with a strong design sense using a repeat motif.

EXERCISE 1:
MAKING A REPEAT DESIGN:

One of the easiest methods I have found to compose a design is to use a single, simple silhouette and repeat. Recalling the traditional quilt block, you will realize how easy this is to do and how pleasing the results are.

Start by choosing a simple object that has a pleasing shape to act as your model. This could be a figurine of an animal, a bird, or a child's toy. One suggestion is to draw the image upside down. This objectifies it so you see the whole as the shape that you want to reproduce, as opposed to seeing the object as something specific. Hold the object or place it on a base of plasticine upside down. This should give you a fresh perspective in attempting to draw it.

Draw only the outline or silhouette of the solid figure. When you have completed the drawing, turn it right side up. If it is recognizable as the object you want to draw, then you are finished. It does not have to be an exact replica. An original rendition can be charming and fresh.

Glue your finished drawing to stiff card paper or light cardboard. Cut it out to use as a template. Using your template as a pattern, draw more silhouettes, preferably on different colored construction paper. Cut these out and randomly place them on a larger sheet of paper. Now, play with the design by overlapping to create dimension, flop them to reverse their direction, place lighter colors in front of darker colors and so on. The playful gathering of ducks arranged at left is an example of how this process can yield an appealing design.

When you've reached a point at which you're pleased with what you've created, dab your silhouette shapes with a little glue to keep them in place on the sheet of paper and pin up to use as a guide to your fabric piece.

Now again using your template, or perhaps blowing it up to a larger size (enlarging photocopiers are perfect, inexpensive, and readily available), you can begin your work in fabric.

There are many methods from which you can choose to finish this work. For *The Ugly Duckling*, the ducks are outlined with machine-quilting; the beaks are appliquéd; the feet are embroidered; the swan is appliquéd; and in the background I experimented with crayons.

For this exercise, I suggest you try using a paper transfer adhesive, Wonder-Under™ for easy machine-appliqué. Again using your template, trace as many silhouettes as you require on the paper side of the Wonder-Under™ Remember that the image you trace will be reversed

when attached to the fabric so you might want to turn over your template now.

Cut the images out of the Wonder-Under™ leaving some excess space around your drawings at this time. Iron these images onto the reverse sides of a variety of fabrics. Now trim and peel away the paper part of the Wonder-Under™ Arrange these fabric shapes on a background fabric according to your design and iron into place. The work is now ready for machine-appliqué.

Arrange the duck shapes into a playful composition. (Play with the duck shapes on a background sheet until you have an arrangement that satisfies you.)

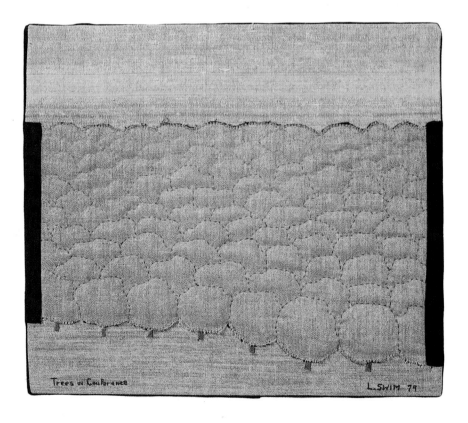

Above: The single image is reversed and repeated in this paper cut-out fantasy of **Dancers,** *by Ann Bird.*
Above right: Playful interaction happens when a single object composed of simple shapes in fabric is repeated in a toss-around fashion. Sheila Ladislao was ten years old when she did this in an "Artist in the School Program" in which I taught. Below right: In **Trees in Conference,** *I used the simple shape of a circle in repeat, mostly indicated by quilting, to portray a forest.*

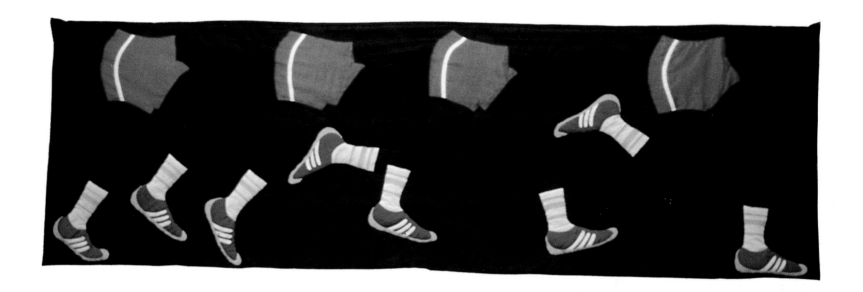

Above: After making a group of the same shapes, you can create a focus by putting in another view of the subject you have chosen to work with. **Runners,** by Ann Bird, is composed of two major shapes in repeat.
Left: **The Ugly Duckling,** by Laurie Swim.

*Left: In **Red Shoe**, by Laurie Swim, the building, a dominant part of the composition, touches two sides of the border. Right: In **Off Shore**, by Laurie Swim, dividing the negative space is as important as the positive shapes, the ship and the land.*

EXERCISE 2:
CREATING A PICTORIAL
COMPOSITION:

This method can be used for designing quilt blocks for an album quilt, centerpieces for a single-image quilt with borders, or pictures in fabric.

Start by making a viewfinder. Take a piece of paper or thin cardboard—cut in the same shape as the final format you are going to work with—and draw two lines diagonally from corner to corner, crossing in the middle.

With a pencil, place a dot on each of the four lines one inch (2.5 cm) from the center. Connect the dots. The resulting rectangle will exactly mirror the shape of your piece. Cut out the rectangle to complete your viewfinder.

Close one eye. Hold the viewfinder a short distance from your open eye and use it to scan the room for interesting compositions. The viewfinder is a perceptual window that frames your shapes.

Beginners tend to pile up their subject in the center of their composition; therefore, as a general rule, if you have chosen a single object as your subject, it should touch at least two sides of your viewfinder and therefore touch the borders of

your drawing at two places. The same applies if you choose a cluster of objects or a still life. By using the viewfinder, you determine the relationship of space to the format. The negative space is space around an object and is as important as the positive space, which consists of the solid objects. One of the essential elements of composition is a balance between negative and positive space.

Now that you've chosen what you're going to draw, we will proceed with how to draw it. Use a soft pencil, 2B or 4B, rather than a hard one and a piece of plain white paper, such as typing paper. Do not choose a shiny surface because pencil marks smudge. Look at your subject through your viewfinder, one eye closed, to flatten the surfaces in the composition. Before starting the drawing, mentally note where the objects in your composition touch the sides of the viewfinder.

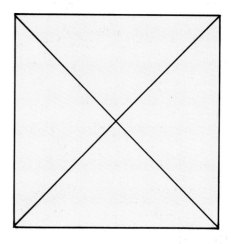

Draw two lines diagonally from corner to corner dissecting the middle.

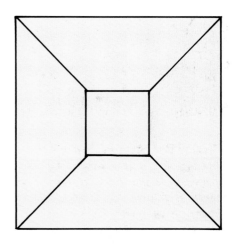

Draw a box intersecting the cross, reflecting the same shape as the outside edge of the paper. Cut out for your viewfinder.

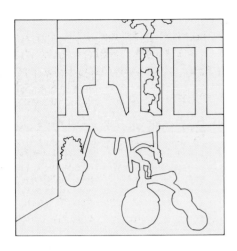

Looking at the negative space and drawing it uses the right hemisphere of your brain.

Connect lines to complete the shape and keep details to a minimum.

Only look at the negative spaces in relationship to the boundaries of the viewfinder. Seeing the "empty space" as shapes uses the right hemisphere of your brain. These are the shapes you draw.

When you have completed drawing the negative spaces you see within the viewfinder, you will see the beginning of the whole picture as it is taking shape. Join the lines around your shapes at this time, making corrections as necessary. Put some detail in your positive shapes, but keep them simple. You will surprise yourself with the results. And the more you practice, the better you will get.

These are all methods I first learned in art school and are covered in more detail in Betty Edwards' *Drawing on the Right Side of the Brain*. Think of this drawing in the patterns, textures, and colors of fabrics. Exciting, isn't it?

Now you must choose fabric and color. Next you will render your drawing, which if you used typing paper is approximately 8.5 x 11 inches (21 x 27.5 cm), in a collage of colored shapes. If it pleases at this size it is then a simple matter to enlarge it for your finished work. This is the guide for your selection of fabrics.

For the next step you need colored bits of paper, both patterned and plain. If you have access to a variety of origami papers, buy them. They come in small, beautiful patterns like calico fabric and also in plain colors. The sheets are usually small and are sold in packages. They can be pieced together to make a larger shape. You can also collect wrapping paper, either plain or featuring small prints. I also have a collection of sample books of small-print wallpaper.

Should you have a large collection of fabric ("The one with the most scraps of fabric when she dies, wins") by all means make a selection and try various combinations at this size. Don't worry about scale yet. Wonder-Under™ scraps, fabric, or paper glue can act as the adhesive.

Next, take a sheet of tracing paper the size of your drawing and trace your drawing. Set the original drawing aside. Take a piece of carbon paper and tape it black side up on the table. Place the tracing of your drawing over the carbon paper, taping the upper left corner to the surface. Choose a shape in the drawing, select a colored or patterned paper or fabric scrap, and place it between the tracing and the carbon, colored side up. Trace out the first desired shape. This is best done with a dried ball-point pen. The carbon paper will transfer an outline of the shape to the reverse side of the paper or fabric.

Slide out the colored paper or fabric. Turn it over. The first shape is ready to cut. Repeat with the next shape. Where one shape abuts another, leave an overlap so you can tuck the first shape under the one on top.

When all the shapes are cut out, assemble your collage on a background paper and tack it with glue. You now have a scale model, or maquette, of the work in progress and a guide for the final selection of fabrics.

At this point I pin up the maquette and step back from it. Problems that are not apparent on a flat surface will leap out when you look at the design on the wall. If you see a problem, don't be discouraged.

Try a few different solutions. If you think the composition is weak, cut out two oversize right angles from cardboard and frame the piece differently, moving in and out by degrees. Step back and take a hard look. You'll be astonished at how much the work changes. This will also give you several versions of your work.

If you think that color is the problem, cut out a few different combinations of fabric and color to lay over what you have. If necessary, move some of the shapes around. It might occur to you to

add something extra, a touch that will make the piece work for you.

When working on *Pears*, I struggled for some time with the maquette, until I realized that the piece needed the insects to complete it. When you have completed this process to your complete satisfaction, you are ready to enlarge your drawing and make the finished piece.

Where the Heart Is... is a 14-x-14-inch (35-x-35-cm) quilt block that began as a design for a large wall hanging, but when my local guild announced a competition for an appliqué quilt block, I decided it would be a good exercise for me to work on a variety of strict, traditional hand-sewing techniques.

I also wanted to create a three-dimensional effect using patterned fabric. Note the angle of the pattern in the fabric that gives perspective to the brick wall on the left side of the picture.

The trees were a challenge as well. I had to cut through three layers of fabric using reverse appliqué to create the underbranches of the blue fir. I learned to handle frayed edges and resolved the problems created by tiny corners with a white liquid called Fray-No-More™ that dries clear, specifically manufactured to prevent fraying.

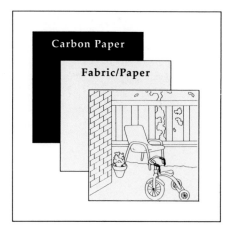

Tape carbon paper, black side up, to surface. Place traced drawing on top. Between drawing and carbon, slip in choice of fabric (or paper) under the desired shape. Trace over desired shape. The image will appear on the wrong side of the fabric (or paper). Cut out the shape. Continue. When one shape abuts another, leave an overlap so that it can be tucked under shape in front.

*Maquette in paper of **Where the Heart is...***

Once the sewing of the appliqué surface was finished and the filler and backing put together, I proceeded with the quilting. With so many layers in a small area—for example, where the fence overlapped the tree—I had to quilt in stab stitches, rather than a running stitch, resulting in a rather erratic underside.

This particular scene was taken from a view through the door of our second-floor apartment. The doorway acted as the viewfinder. I eventually turned the square into a cushion cover. On the other side of the cushion I quilted the title. It is a memory gift to my young son and really should be part of a larger album quilt. I'll keep an open book on this as a project, and by the time my son Jacob, now four years old, is an adult, it will be a completed quilt.

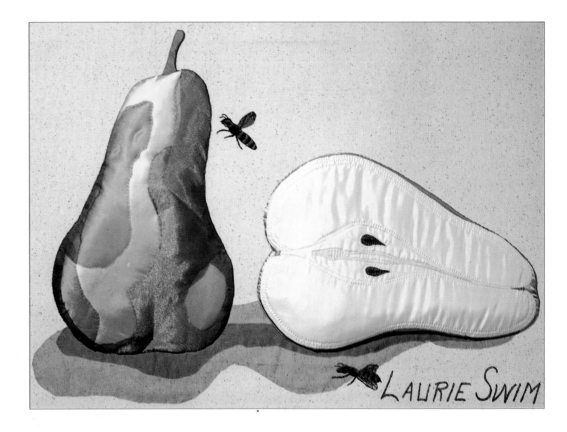

A Gallery of Appliqué Quilts

A Marriage *measures 80 by 40 inches (200 by 100 cm). I used overlays and underlays of organza and opaque silk to make the subtle changes in this landscape. The nude figure of the woman, for instance, is created by a peach fabric under the white silk and distinguished from the foreground by a quilted line. The top of the figure is then appliquéd to the background. The sections that divide the format represent a hexagon from* **I Ching, The Book of Changes.**

I Remember Summerville *measures 30 by 40 inches (75 by 100 cm). The sea in this work is hand-quilted satin; the wave is machine stitched with a shirred silk white-cap. I made the foamy shallow water in the fore-ground from an overlay of pulled cheesecloth. Padded faced appliqué shapes make up the figure.*

Family Album, *by Doris Waddell.*
The composition of the imagery in the pictorial blocks on this album quilt is cleanly executed in delightfully appropriate fabrics. The attention to detail is used to accentuate without becoming fussy. The alternate blocks of larger motifs provide adequate spacing between the story blocks and strengthen the impact of the overall design, which measures 90 by 90 inches or 225 by 225 cm.

Gardens on the Hill, *by Angelika Kraus-Werth. This work (measuring 64 by 72 inches, or 160 by 180 cm) finds strength as a whole in the repeat shades of houses and trees. Upon closer inspection, the attention to detail is a visual feast.*

Hawthorne Hill, *by D. Joyce Davies. Beautifully rendered flowers in bold colors create the design theme in this appliqué work. Small and large floral shapes in different sized blocks are what hold the viewer's attention and interest.*

Sanctuary—Rainforests Remembered, *by Barb Head, measures 54 by 56 inches (135 by 140 cm). The eagle and fish float within a circle on a machine-stitched textural background. The circle on a square format makes a strong design. Overlays of sheer fabrics create a painterly effect.*

The Tea, *by Rose DiZio measures 24 by 20 inches (60 by 50 cm). A close-up of a scene creates design strength and arranging objects or parts of them becomes important to the composition.*

Baskets, Baskets, *by Jean Evans and Joyce Murrin. The sophisticated composition basically follows an S-curve from the lower left corner taking the eye up through the work, which is 78 by 100 inches (195 by 250 cm). The appliqués are organic shapes that contrast with the piecing, which is angular.*

Moonrise, *by Valerie Hearder measures 48 by 36 inches (120 by 90 cm). Solid, bold colors and shapes create dramatic imagery. Breaking up this scene with two vertical lines helps the viewer focus on the central area of the work.*

Toucans à la Rousseau, *by Dorothy G. Fischer, is a bold colored design, appliquéd and embroidered. The use of a pieced border makes a decorative finish in contrast with the larger shapes of the imagery. It measures 58 by 59 inches (145 by 148 cm).*

CHAPTER THREE

Manipulating Fabric

Any manipulation of fabric is looked upon with great interest. The varied information directly used by the sewer is absorbed in one form or another as part of overall knowledge. Not only in North America, but internationally, there is an exchange of information occurring at conferences and workshops and through informative magazines and books. This is an ongoing process, not likely to stop anytime soon. This sharing of knowledge combined with healthy experimentation will keep the art of quilting alive and thriving.

As more artists use fabric as their mode of expression, there has been more freedom in terms of experimentation and the exploration of it as a creative medium. After I wrote my first book, *The Joy of Quilting,* I realized, through talking with many people, that those interested in working with fabric are also interested in all aspects of needlework.

The reader should be aware that some of the work featured in the gallery sections of this book have undergone such surface treatments as painting, stenciling, dyeing, or batik, and combining media is becoming more popular with fabric artists. In this book, however, we will solely address the manipulation of the surface with fabric treatments.

In this chapter we will look at techniques in fabric that have grown out of the tradition of the crazy quilt, which also combines appliqué and piecework. The principal definition of quilting is the textile sandwich. We will use it as a medium of *bas-relief.* Fabrics are cut and applied to a surface for their visual effect.

Gather together all your scraps and bits and pieces of fabric you haven't been able to throw out for all these years. You'll need a variety of nets, tulles, and lace as well as a pair of sharp scissors, a selection of threads, and your sewing machine.

*Opposite page: Sheer fabrics are used in **Sailing,** by Barb Head, for muted shades and tones, creating a very painterly work that measures 56 by 46 inches (140 by 115 cm).*

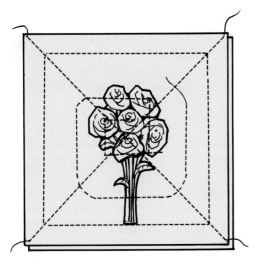

Loosely cut flower petal shapes out of colored scraps arranged on a fabric background. Add netting and baste.

Right: **Mountain Bouquet.** *I used fresh picked flowers for inspiration.*

EXERCISE 1:
A FABRIC BOUQUET

In the first exercise, the subject will be a bouquet of flowers (see Mountain Bouquet). *To facilitate creativity, treat yourself to a bouquet of flowers. A fresh flower arrangement, as a still life, is always an inspiration.*

Select a background fabric or combination of fabrics a little larger than you want your finished work to be. Choose soft fabrics. The sample here is velveteen. Place your background on layers of padding and backing. I prefer interfacing fleece, a thick, felted fabric for the padding. Select fabric scraps appropriate in texture and color for the flowers. Use your scissors as your drawing tool—neither patterns nor templates are necessary for this exercise.

Loosely cut flower petal shapes out of your various colored scraps, and arrange them on your background. To create shaded areas in the petals of your flowers, lay on small amounts of tulle net. Don't worry about specific shapes; the

tulle can be trimmed later. Put in bits and pieces for pistils and stamens. Then cut out leaves and apply them.

When the arrangement pleases you, cover the piece, including the entire background, with the larger-spaced netting (not the tulle). Choose a color that best suits the overall hues of the flowers.

Pin and baste the layers thoroughly. Adjust your sewing machine so that it takes the layers and still moves freely. Lower your feed dogs and start by sewing the flowers—catching the fabric and outlining the petals, crossing them several times—all in a running stitch to trap the work underneath.

When you have done this to the

flowers, buds, and leaves, draw in your stems and stalks with chalk to guide you and sew either by straight-stitching repeatedly or by satin-stitching.

Having finished the sewing to your satisfaction, simply cut away the heavier netting from the areas you wish to highlight. The remaining netting should enhance your design. The netting is mainly used to stabilize the bits of fabric while they are being sewed down.

Pin it up. Stand back. Assess pluses and minuses. Subtract by clipping out fabric with embroidery snips. Make additions by layering more fabric and net. You have begun to learn a new mode of expression in fabric.

EXERCISE 2:
FABRIC SKETCHING

The following exercise will take you further into this technique.
I call it fabric sketching.

Draw a scene, using your newfound skills learned in Chapter Two, or choose a favorite photo or select a picture you have cut from a magazine. Some students use paintings of the Old Masters to study techniques.

Having chosen your subject matter, you will use virtually the same principles as in Exercise 1 in this chapter, only this time the decision making will be a little more complex. For instance, you may choose a variety of netting to overlay your selection of fabrics, making different colors work for you in tone and texture. (See *Community,* by the author, for example.)

For fabric sketches I start with a layer of muslin backing, padding of Insulite™, interfacing fleece and add my background fabrics, such as silk or blue cotton for the sky, and a foreground of any number of different fabrics. All are cut freehand. Each piece has rough edges.

I go on to cut shapes to represent trees, buildings, animals, and so on. This is overlaid with the netting and secured with straight pins.

Pin up the work-in-progress to review and revise. When the work pleases you, baste thoroughly and begin sewing on the machine as in the previous exercise. Don't be afraid to draw with the machine as you sew and quilt the piece.

Begin to trim net where you want true colors to be pronounced. Leave the net in place where shading or muted tones are preferred.

Pin up the work once again. Using the viewfinder you constructed in Chapter Two, frame the composition to discover where your borders fit best.

For finishing you might want to use beads or embroidery as accents, but remember to go easy on your embellishing.

*Left: Photograph of the Grand Tetons.
Below: Fabric rendition of the
Grand Tetons.*

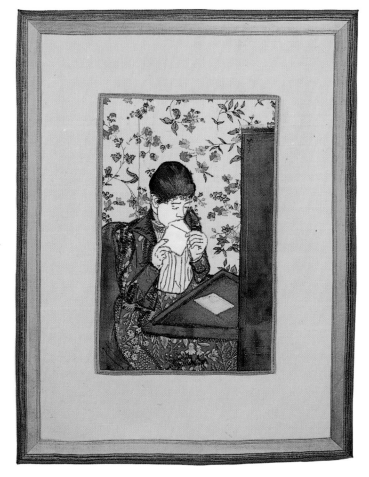

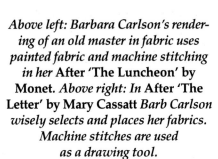

Above left: Barbara Carlson's rendering of an old master in fabric uses painted fabric and machine stitching in her **After 'The Luncheon' by Monet.** *Above right: In* **After 'The Letter' by Mary Cassatt** *Barb Carlson wisely selects and places her fabrics. Machine stitches are used as a drawing tool.*

Community *is one of four panels I designed for Co-operator's Data Services. Many employees, both male and female volunteered their time to sew the panels. A variety of innovative techniques were used. Each panel is 90 by 40 inches (225 by 100 cm).*

FROM AN IDEA TO A FINISHED WORK

To take some of the mystery out of the process of making a complex piece, I am going to take you through the stages of the construction of my work Early Spring.

For years the giant American elm at the corner of our block intrigued me, especially our view of it. We lived in a second-floor apartment, and from our front balcony we watched it change with the seasons. Its natural beauty was as astonishing as it was welcome, for we lived at that time amid the concrete and traffic in the center of a large, modern city. It was at least 75 feet (22.5 m) tall and a century old. It not only survived the polluted air, it wasn't ravaged by Dutch elm disease. It still stands. I think of it as a monument to the life will of nature.

For three years I took photos of the tree through all the seasons. It was the early spring view that I finally chose to do as a quilt. The new buds gave the tree a glow, without hiding the strength of limb structure or the sky behind it.

I started with a small sketch. Working from the sketch and a photograph, I then made a larger drawing with conté and washes to portray the spirit I wanted to capture.

From there I moved on to make a cartoon—a full-size sketch on brown paper—of the tree's trunk and basic network of branches. I placed a large sheet of tracing paper on top of the cartoon and outlined the tree.

I added the tracing paper to a layer of off-white opaque silk backed by an aqua-colored broadcloth, basting all three together. I then machine-sewed the paper to the layers of cloth, following the lines of the traced drawing. This done, I removed the paper and trimmed the aqua broadcloth to effect a glowing sky.

Afterward, I filled in the trunk and larger branches with fabric strips and ribbons as well as added texture to the trunk with running and satin stitches. After pinning this to the wall, I drew the web of small branches that appear in the finished work directly onto the cloth freehand. For this I used a disappearing ink pen. I only made a few lines at a time, removing the work from the wall and filling in these branches with satin

stitch on the machine, starting thick and tapering to a thin line. I repeated this process until I had a natural-looking network of branches.

I wanted the background to take a secondary place in the final work so I decided on a collage of muted fabrics and shapes to represent the more distant landscape and buildings. To portray early evening, the time when the setting sun is reflected in the windows of facing buildings, I used the yellow-gold satin. The evergreen was cut freehand out of a green wool and overlaid with black lace to achieve the right effect.

At this point I added a layer of Insulite™ padding, which I basted and then machine-quilted around the trunk and various shapes to create a three-dimensional effect.

Next, I added our balcony railing slats, which were made of folded hand-dyed cotton, and straight-stitched it at the top in order to create a shadow effect. I then added the horizontal edge of the railing by binding the top of the folded fabric. The birds were assembled from an old silk tie with a bit of embroidery; then they were hand-stitched to the piece as a final touch.

The view of the American elm that became the fabric work, **Early Spring.**

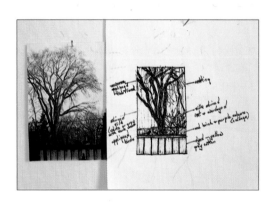

A small compositional sketch was the first step.

A larger sketch with conte and washes captured the mood of the piece.

Brown paper was used to make a full-scale drawing or cartoon of the tree.

The drawing was transferred to a layer of light silk and turquoise broadcloth. The trunk and branches were filled in with fabric.

Smaller branches were done in satin stitch, starting thick and tapering to a thin line.

Bright yellow-gold fabric was used for the sun-reflecting windows. A collage of other fabrics represents distant scenery. The birds were made from an old silk tie.

The evergreen was cut from green wool fabric and overlaid with black lace.

CHAPTER FOUR

Learning the
Fundamentals

The following is a basic checklist of equipment you will need to start quilting. If you are a sewer, you probably have most of these things on hand and will only have to make a few additions. If you are just beginning, you can find most of these items in a notions department, fabric store, or crafts shop.

NEEDLES AND PINS

Keep a selection of Sharps™ needles. Numbers 8 and 9 are fine and useful for most hand-sewing needs.

Long and short straight pins are both needed for quilting. Glass-head pins are useful sometimes as a substitute for basting a hand-quilted piece.

THREADS

Buy threads to suit the fabrics you intend to use: cotton for cottons, polyester blends for cotton-polyesters. It is a good idea to keep on hand large spools of black and neutral gray.

In addition, keep spools of red, yellow, green, and several shades of blue, as there is a broad range of blue to be used. This selection should cover most situations, but when buying fabric for a specific project, it is advisable to match the thread at the same time. If you cannot match the color, it is safer to purchase thread a shade darker than the fabric being used.

BEESWAX

Beeswax is not essential, but it is especially nice for hand-sewing, including quilting with the stiffer quilting thread. You just pull your thread through the solid piece of wax before stitching. It strengthens the thread and helps it slip more easily through the fabric. You should be able to find beeswax in the notions section of the fabric store.

THIMBLE

It is important to learn to use a thimble if you are doing a lot of hand-sewing. It should fit comfortably on the second finger of your sewing hand. Use it to push the needle through the fabric and back up to the surface, using a rocking motion. When quilting, the beginner should bandage the second finger of the sewing hand, which is used to guide the needle under the quilt.

SCISSORS AND ROTARY CUTTERS

It is worth your while to invest in a good, lightweight pair of fabric scissors that you use only for cutting fabric. When selecting a pair of scissors, make sure the tips meet perfectly. Because this is probably your single most important tool in fabric work, you should be sure to purchase scissors of good quality. Some sewers won't allow anyone else to use their scissors for fear that another person's different hand pressure will upset the instrument's balance. Think of this tool as an extension of your hand.

Rotary cutters are very useful for cutting a number of layers of fabric at the same time and for cutting long strips of material. They should always be used with special cutting boards so as to preserve the blade.

RULERS

When buying a yardstick or meter rule, select one that is made of metal or plastic rather than wood, because wood tends to warp over time. A metal ruler is good for cutting lines with a rotary knife. A dressmaker ruler is made of clear, see-through plastic. Right-angled or T-square rulers are used when it is necessary to make right angles or forty-five-degree corners.

PENS AND PENCILS

Keep a collection of felt tip pens and hard and soft pencils on hand for making patterns and designs in paper. Colored pencils and tailor's pencils are acceptable for marking fabric, but hurrah for the recent development of pencils that make marks that can be wiped off with a damp cloth. In addition to these "erasable" pencils, there is a felt-tipped pen equipped with disappearing ink. I find this useful for drawing freehand, quilting lines, and embroidering on the machine. Be sure to test these disappearing pens on scraps of the fabric you intend to use in your work to make sure they won't leave a stain after disappearing.

IRON

Steam irons are the best for pressing seams. Whatever iron you use, however, always iron with a pressing cloth so your fabrics don't become shiny.

SEWING MACHINE

Your machine should make a good, even straight stitch, my personal experience being that in older models, machines only capable of straight stitch are best for making a good running stitch. Machines with decorative stitches, even if that only means zigzag, tend not to make as good a straight stitch because of the movement of the needle. I have two older-model machines, both good workhorses; one I use for creating straight stitch and the other for satin stitch.

There are, however, new machines on the market capable of accomplishing any number of stitches admirably, so consider these if you wish to invest in a top-of-the-line sewing machine.

FABRICS

All fabrics should be washed before becoming part of your quilt. This will not only remove the sizing—a stiffener manufacturers put in to give the fabric body—and allow easier cutting and sewing, but it preshrinks the fabric if it is prone to this problem. Also, washing will make the fabrics uniform for handling.

For piecework and appliqué, dress-weight one hundred percent cotton is best due to its manageability. Polyester-cotton blends are considered less desirable because they have a springiness that doesn't press into a crisp seam. You may wish to experiment with silks, satins, velvets, and brocades, which can create wonderful effects.

Scraps and used fabrics appeal to our sense of economy and perhaps history and have a special patina and charm. They should not be used, however, in a utilitarian object in which they may wear out too quickly. I like old silk ties with wild patterns, for example, to play with. Most people avoid stretchy fabrics because they are difficult to sew. Wools are lovely but are generally thought of as too thick for quilting.

Keep in mind there are no rules, and you should experiment on your own to achieve whatever effects you are looking for. It is best to be aware of a fabric's possibilities and then go about using it to your best advantage.

FILLERS

Polyester and Dacron™ batting are what most quilters use today as fillers in the textile sandwich. There are different weights and thicknesses, and these are used depending on the effects you wish to achieve. Generally, the thicker they are the harder it is to hand-quilt.

A word of caution: Check the label to make sure the batting is bonded or glazed. This will prevent *bearding,* which is when the batting migrates through the surface of the fabric, a most unpleasant effect.

There are other kinds of fillers. The cotton batt is denser, and some quilters prefer it because it is made of natural fiber. You have to be careful using it, however, because if it is not quilted thoroughly, the cotton shifts and lumps with washing and wear.

Wool batt is comparable to polyester batt in that both have some of the same qualities of thickness, and, of course, there is added warmth. It is not always readily available and needs to be cold-water-washed, so may not be good for use on a child's bed, for example.

Insulite™, or polyester interfacing fleece, is a flat, compact filler or padding used as liner for winter coats and is especially nice for use in quilted wall hangings. It pads without creating a too-puffy surface and is very easy to hand- or machine-quilt.

FRAMES AND HOOPS

Frames or bars are usually formed from four wooden boards, two long and two short. The textile sandwich is rolled on the longer bars and laced to the crossbars. Quilting frames and bars are used by serious quilters with a lot of space to work in—a group or a guild, for example, which meets on a regular basis in a hall or space set aside for them. The big advantage in using quilting bars is that you are more likely to end up with evenly shaped quilts.

Quilting hoops are generally used because of their portability. They measure about 24 inches (60 cm) in diameter and are of heavier construction than embroidery hoops. As well as being used for quilting, they are useful for holding fabric taut while doing appliqué.

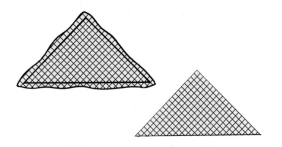

Draw the geometric shape on graph paper. Cut out, leaving some excess space.

Piecing is also known as patchwork and refers to joining small irregular shapes together with seams. For hand piecing especially, one hundred percent cotton dress weight is best because it is the easiest to manage. Fabrics used should generally be of the same weight and texture.

TEMPLATES

Templates are best drawn on graph paper first so that the geometric shape is worked out correctly. Glue the paper with the shape on it to card paper, and cut out the shape with an X-Acto™ knife and metal ruler. Scissors are not as precise.

For hand-piecing:

• Cut out one template with a seam allowance and one without. Remove the selvage from the fabric with a rotary knife and board.

• Lay the fabric on a flat surface, wrong side up. From the previously cut line, starting at one end, place the larger tem-

Left: Glue the graph paper to a stiffer card stock. Right: Trim shape precisely with an X-Acto knife.

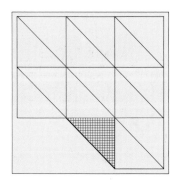

Place the template on fabric and trace around it as many times as needed.

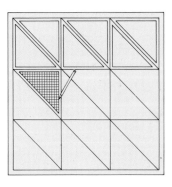

For seam allowance, place the small template in the middle of the shape, and trace.

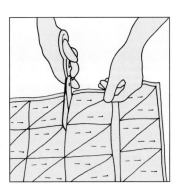

Several layers of fabric can be cut at one time if the top marked fabric is pinned carefully to the other layers.

plate on the fabric and draw around it. Continue drawing a series of these shapes, fitting one flush against the other on the fabric. Place the smaller template in the middle of your drawn shapes and draw around it. Slant the marker tip away from the template, to get as close as possible to the size desired.

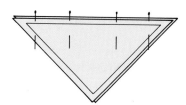

Pin first at each end and then the middle of one side of the shape.

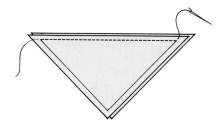

Be careful not to sew into the seam allowance in hand piecing.

For machine-piecing:

• Make only one template with a seam allowance. When piecing by machine, use your pressure foot for a guide for the seam allowance. Proceed to make your fabric shapes in the same way as previously discussed.

PIECING METHODS

If you are *hand-piecing*, pin the fabric pieces, right sides together, first at each end and then in the middle of one side of the shape to prevent fabric from shifting. Pins should be placed at right angles to the seam allowance.

Thread a needle from the spool, then cut it and knot it at the end you just cut. This will ensure that the twist of the thread is going in the right direction: with the sewing, not against it.

Do not sew into the seam allowance in hand-piecing. Sew by starting at a corner where the two lines of the seam allowances meet, and end at the other corner by taking a few backstitches. As you sew, check to see that you are following the guidelines on both sides.

After joining pieces, iron the seams of the hand-pieced patches not open but over to one side. This makes the piece-work stronger.

If you are *machine-piecing*, place right sides together, with pins at right angles to the seam, as before. Sew on the machine, ten or twelve stitches to the inch (2.5 cm) from edge to edge, removing pins as you go.

By leaving a short length of thread between each set, you can sew a series of patches and separate them afterward. Once they are separated, iron the seams open before continuing the assembly.

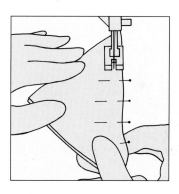

For machine piecing place pins at right angles to the sewing line and remove pins as you go.

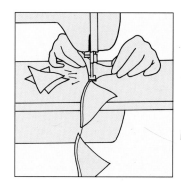

Leaving a short length of thread between sets, sew patches in a series and separate afterwards.

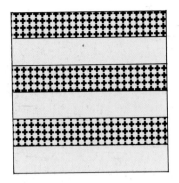

Bands of different-colored fabrics are sewn together.

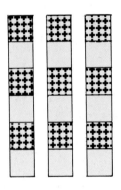

Bands sewn together are cut into vertical strips.

STRIP-PIECING

Strip-piecing, also known as Seminole patchwork, is best done on a sewing machine. It is a technique originated by the Seminole Indians of Florida and was used to create brightly colored geometric patterns for accenting yokes and cuffs of clothing. The finished appearance looks a lot more complicated than it really is. It is a method that breaks up fabric into strips, which are reassembled into new yardage from which the designer creates a more complex surface. In recent years this technique has been explored as a creative expression extensively and freely, as seen in the many examples in Chapter One.

It is helpful to have a preliminary understanding of some of the basic, original Seminole methods of developing small, patterned pieces. Strips of different colors are cut and sewn together. Once sewn, the reassembled fabric is cut vertically across the strips to create new strips. By simply reversing the order of every other newly cut strip and sewing these together, you can create a checker-board fabric.

Alternatively, by dropping each strip one square to meet the corner of the next square, a diamond pattern can be created. By trimming top, bottom, and sides, one can fabricate a new cloth. This gives you the gist of the process and an inkling of the numerous variations you can achieve. By varying just the width of your cut strip, for example, the pattern changes phenomenally from the simple structure just demonstrated.

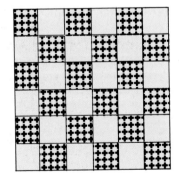

Reversing the order creates a checker-board fabric.

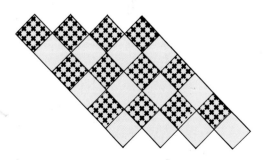

Dropping each strip one square creates a diamond pattern.

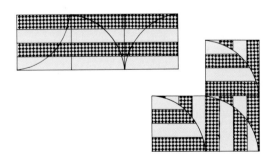

Shapes are cut from the strip-pieced fabric, then rearranged to create interesting new patterns.

Simple, traditional patterns, such as the nine-patch block, (see Chapter One, page 18) and pieced medallion patterns, such as the Bethlehem or Texas star, become more manageable when strip-pieced.

In contemporary quilting, this is an ongoing process whose myriad possibilities are still being explored. For a wonderful example of free expression in strip-piecing, see *The Guardians*, by Erika Carter, on page 20.

Strip-piecing is very popular for the exploration of color gradations, from dark to light and vice versa. You may wish to dye your own fabrics to achieve a specific or wide range of shades. Template shapes cut out of strip-pieced fabric can fit together to form a completely new and original pattern.

Above: **Star of Bethlehem,** *quilt from the Shelburne Museum. Left:* **Letting Go,** *by Miriam Nathan-Roberts, portrays undulating ribbons made of dyed fabrics strip-pieced in graduated shades of blue.*

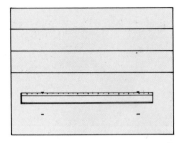

Measure and mark the strips parallel to the selvage with a ruler.

Several layers can be cut at one time. Carefully pin the top marked fabric to the layers underneath it.

NOTES FOR BASIC STRIP-PIECING

• Strips should be cut, not torn, for easier piecing.

• Strips longer than 54 inches (135 cm) are awkward and hard to handle.

• When deciding the finished width of a strip, always add a seam allowance. Strips should not be less than 1 inch (2.5 cm), or seams on either side get in the way. If you want a strip thinner than 1 inch (2.5 cm), use piping or a printed or woven striped fabric to achieve the effect you want instead of strip-piecing.

• The selvage edge is most apt to be straight and on the proper grain for cutting. Start at right angles to it, and mark and measure the width of your strip, plus seam allowances, at several points parallel to the selvage. Join these marks with a ruler to get your line for cutting. Continue in this way until you have the number of strips you require.

• Cutting can be done with scissors or rotary knife and cutting board. Several layers can be cut at a time if the top layer only is marked. To do this, pin the marked fabric carefully to the other layers. Place the pins in the middle of each marked strip.

• It is not necessary to mark seam allowances when piecing on the machine. Use your pressure foot as a guide instead.

• Line up strips, two by two, right sides facing. Pin them periodically to keep them aligned. Sew, removing the pins as you go.

• Line up the assembled strips two by two. Pin and sew as above. You now have a section of four strips, which if you continue become eight, and so on.

• Iron seams open on back, and again on front, when you have completed the sewing of all the strips. You have now created a new fabric surface with which to work.

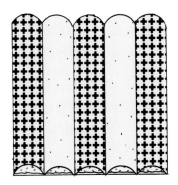

String-quilting can be as simple as sewing a series of colored fabric strips, one at a time, to batting and backing.

Strip-pieced fabric can be recut in strips and string-quilted.

Strip-pieced fabric can be cut at odd angles and string-quilted.

STRING-QUILTING

String-quilting is another facet of strip-piecing. It is a one-step piecing-and-quilting method in which you sew individual strips, the batting, and the backing all at once.

Strips for string-quilting can be as simple as a series of colored fabric strips or strips joined lengthwise or as involved as strip-pieced sections that you have already created, recut into an even more complex surface as well as odd-size straight-edge cut shapes. Whatever method you choose, the principle remains the same.

Odd-sized straight-edged shapes can be assembled with string-quilting.

NOTES ON STRING-QUILTING

• Use a backing fabric of medium or heavy weight, or starch a lighter fabric to stiffen it. This precaution will help prevent the backing from moving around when you are sewing the strips and give a more striking relief effect to the front surface.

• Cut backing fabric into 20-inch (50-cm) widths. There is a limit to how much bulk you can handle under the neck of your sewing machine. The length can be rolled in your lap with each pass of the stitching, but the width can become awkward and uncontrollable. Avoid this problem by dividing the quilt into manageable sections to be assembled as a whole later.

Baste the batting to the backing through the center area and around the perimeter one-quarter inch (6 mm) from the edge. That will eventually become the seam line. Trim the batting to the seam line close to the basting. This eliminates bulk in the seams and makes joining the finished pieces easier later on.

• Your cut strips of surface fabric should not be too narrow, especially if this is your first try. Narrow strips tend to flatten the batting, and spoil the bas-relief effect. Too wide strips also flatten the batting, but you can overcome this by using a double thickness of filler.

• Pin both sides of the first strip to the batting and backing, and sew on the sewing machine. You should try to use

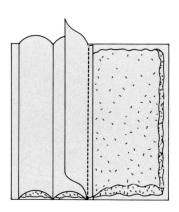

Attach the fabric strip to the preceding one, sewing through the batting and backing in one step.

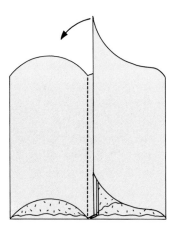

Method 1: To join the sections discreetly, leave the seams of one section unsewn. Leaving the back open, sew the front side to the seams of the other section.

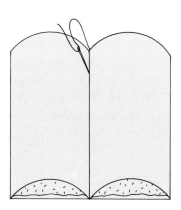

Finish by hand-sewing the back side of the section to cover the other trimmed seams.

your zipper foot on your machine, as it will not catch in the batting as readily as will the pressure foot. Another precaution is to place a strip of scrap paper under the right side of the foot to cover and press the batting away from the needle as you sew.

• Place the next strip on top of the first, right sides together; pin at the right-hand seam line; and sew ten to twelve stitches to the inch (2.5 cm), removing the pins as you go. Turn out second strip; pin the

third strip as before and continue.

• When you've come to the last strip in each section, consider these two methods of joining the sections:

(a) Do not stitch down the last side of the last strip. Fold back the backing and batting, and pin it out of the way. Pin the unfinished strip along the seam line to the front left side of another section. Sew them together on the machine. Trim the seam allowance. Fold the backing over the exposed seam, turning the edge under,

and hand-stitch in place. This should discreetly hide the joins.

(b) This method is not quite so elegant, but does the job. Finish all seams. Place sections together, two at a time, front surfaces facing each other. Add a strip of fabric about 1.5 inches (4 cm) wide to one side of the two sections. Pin these layers, and sew on the machine. Trim the seam. Fold the strip over the seam, turning under the edge, and hand-stitch in place.

Method 2: Place two sections together so the top sides are facing. Add a strip of fabric to one side of the seam and sew on the machine. Trim.

Fold the strip over the seam. Turn under and finish by hand.

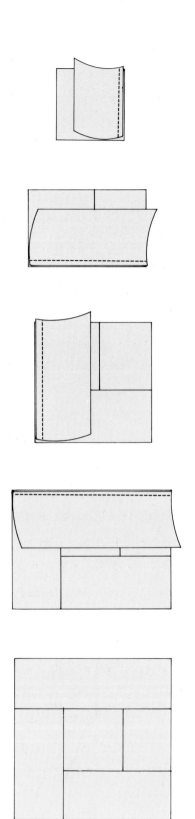

Log cabin quilt from the Shelburne Museum demonstrates the use of dark and light in the individual square that creates a vibrant overall pattern.

Log cabin piecing sequence.

Courthouse steps piecing sequence.

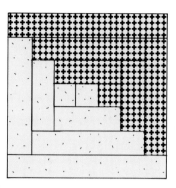

Contrasts in log cabin block.

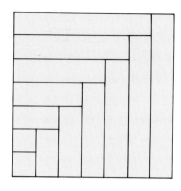

Vary the log cabin pattern by placing the square in the lower left corner.

LOG CABIN AND COURTHOUSE STEPS BLOCKS

These two traditional blocks are as versatile in design and construction as strip-piecing and can be handled in much the same manner within a block design. Traditionally they are pieced as strips in block form, compiled as a quilt top, then quilted as a textile sandwich or, as demonstrated here, made into individual completed blocks in the quilt-as-you-go string-quilted method.

The log cabin and courthouse steps patterns traditionally start with a square in the center. In the log cabin design, the quilter adds a strip to one side of the square, then places a strip to the long side of these two pieces together, and continues in that mode. In the courthouse steps design, the quilter adds strips to opposite sides of the square, then places longer strips on opposite sides of that construction, and so on.

The variations can be as simple as contrasting-color arrangements or as detailed as patterns using strips of varied widths and centerpieces of different shapes and placements. Myriad patterns can also be created by the arrangement of the repeated blocks in the quilt top.

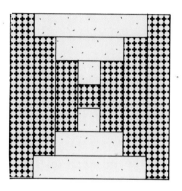

Contrasts in courthouse steps block.

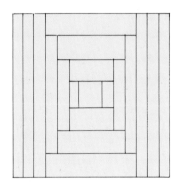

Vary the width of the strips as in this courthouse steps block.

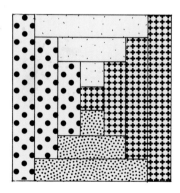

Various contrasting shades in courthouse steps.

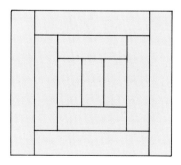

Change the center square to a rectangle, as in this example of courthouse steps.

NOTES ON QUILT-AS-YOU-GO METHODS FOR LOG CABIN AND COURTHOUSE STEPS BLOCKS

• The backing and batting for each quilt are put together in much the same way that they would be for a string-quilted section, as described on page 87. The difference is that the backing fabric of your quilt block should be marked as a guide. Either you can draw an X with pencil so you can see it through the batting, or you can sew an X through the backing and batting, which will hold these two layers together.

• The X is a guide that aligns the strips. Start by placing the first piece of fabric over the center of the X on the batting side. This is your center square. Pin it. Add the first strip. Pin, and using the sewing machine, sew one side of the strip to the center square through the batting and backing.

• Continue adding pieces around the center square with the pattern you've chosen until you complete the block. Depending upon the method you choose for joining one quilt block to another, you will stitch the outer edge or leave it open.

• Another method is to piece the block first, iron all seams to one side (preferably out from the center), baste the batting and backing to the top you've created, and machine-quilt on the front, in what is fondly referred to as "stitching in the ditch." This is stitching in the seam lines where the fabric pieces meet. This method can be applied to any machine-pieced work. Remember to always press the seams on the wrong side to one side, do not leave them open. This will add strength to the finished work.

For the most part all of these procedures can be adapted to the various piecing techniques. Once you master these simpler piecing methods, you will find new ways of challenging yourself and developing your own.

Illustrated steps for string-quilting a block.

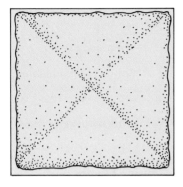

Step 1: The underlayer of the batting and backing of the block should be marked with an X as a guide.

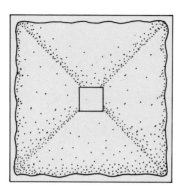

Step 2: Place the fabric square in center, each corner touching the lines of the X. Pin.

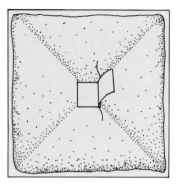

Step 3: Place the first strip to one side of the square and sew on the machine.

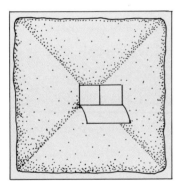

Step 4: Place the next strip and sew, referring to X as a guide.

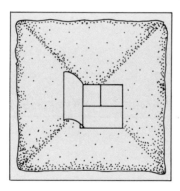

Step 5: Not all strips will start and finish on the X. Refer to the X for alignment just the same. Continue in this way until you reach the sides of the finished block.

Roughly cut out the shape, leaving space around the drawing.

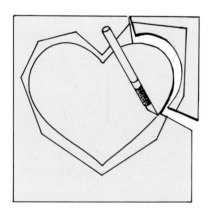

Glue the paper to a thicker card stock and trim with an X-Acto knife.

In appliqué, fabrics of a variety of weights and textures can be mixed and used together to construct the shapes you want. There is no stress caused by the differences as there would be if you used the same mixture of fabrics in piecing, because the appliqué is applied on the top of another surface.

TEMPLATES

Unless you are making your shapes free-hand, you will need a template, or pattern, for cutting out your shape for appliqué accurately.

There are several ways to go about transferring a shape to fabric, depending on the design and the type of appliqué.

• You will first need a drawing of the image. If the image is repeated, a regular template is necessary. To make the template, cut around the drawing, glue it to card paper, and trim to the outline of the shape. This method is used in both machine- and hand-appliqué.

• Alternately, if the design is composed of several different images to comprise a whole picture, make a tracing of the drawing first. With dressmaker carbon paper, transfer the shapes, one at a time, to your choice of fabric. Where shapes touch, allow for a little extra overlap on the underneath shape, which will be tucked under the top shape. This method

can be used in completing the exercise in *Where the Heart Is* . . . in Chapter Two. Both machine- and hand-appliqué shapes can be made using this method.

• Another method for transferring shapes to fabric for both the Faced Appliqué (see page 98) and hand-sewn appliqués, which require reinforcement with stay-stitching (see page 96), is to use traced patterns. Simply outline each shape onto tracing paper. Baste this paper with outline to the top surface of the fabric, and sew on the machine, following the outline on the traced drawing. Using the paper, with its drawing as a guide, not only gives an accurate rendition of the design but stabilizes the fabric and makes it easier to sew. Remove the paper by tearing it from the outside toward the stitched line. The paper in the middle section should tear out easily. This method will give you precise shapes for appliqué. Trim the shape with seam allowance to be notched appropriately and tucked under to edge of stitched line.

Notches are cut for convex curves. Straight line and concave curves are straight cuts.

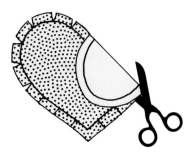

Fold the fabric shape for easy notching.

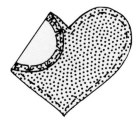

Turning and basting the seam allowance of the appliqué before sewing it to the ground fabric will ensure accuracy.

HAND-APPLIQUÉ

Hand-sewn and machine appliqués are very different. In hand-appliqué, stitches are hidden and the final result is a more fluid line and graceful appearance.

Preparing the Appliqué

• Whatever method you have chosen, remember to add a seam allowance before cutting the shape out of the fabric.

• Cut the shape. Notch the seam allowance appropriately, so that the shape molds easily and smoothly when the seam is turned under. Study the heart shape here as an example of concave and convex lines as well as points and indentations and how they are handled. A

good tip for accurate notching is to fold the seam allowance between your fingers at right angles to the edge while clipping. This gives more control as you cut close to the seam allowance.

• You can further prepare your appliqué by turning and basting the seam allowance before sewing it down to the background. Alternatively, you can baste or pin the shape directly to the background. With your needle, push the edge under and finger-press as you sew down the appliqué. There is a liquid called Fray-No-More™ that prevents sharp cuts, corners, and notches from fraying. It is applied directly to the problem area and dries clear. Use a toothpick, and apply it sparingly. Look for it in the notions department of the fabric store.

Secure the appliqué with pins or basting, and as you go turn the edge under and hand sew.

Position the appliqué with the seam turned and basted on the ground fabric. Baste or pin. It is now ready for fine hand sewing.

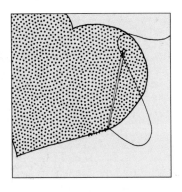

Point the needle down into the ground fabric at the edge of the appliqué.

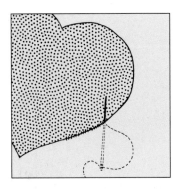

For a hidden stitch, position the tip of the needle into the folded seam edge of the appliqué from the underside.

Sewing the Appliqué

• Place your background fabric in a hoop to keep it taut.

• Begin sewing by burying the knot of the thread in the seam allowance of the appliqué.

• Point the needle straight down into the background, as close to the appliqué as possible. Pull from underneath until thread is snugly seated against the appliqué.

• Come up again in front of the first stitch with only the needle tip showing on the surface, catching the seam line of the shape, not the surface of the appliqué itself.

• Pull taut. Point needle straight down, as before.

• Continue in this way to the end of your thread. Finish by turning the work over, and knotting the thread on the underside of the appliqué in the background fabric layer.

MACHINE-APPLIQUÉ

In machine-appliqué it is not necessary to add a seam allowance unless the fabric from which the shape is cut frays uncontrollably. In this case you will want to stay-stitch, use a fabric adhesive, or make the faced appliqué.

• Cut the shape to be appliquéd from your choice of fabric.

• The traditional method for machine-appliqué is to baste or pin the shape to the background:

(a) Basting should be around the perimeter of the shape and close enough to the edge so as not to interfere with the machine-stitching.

(b) If you are pinning the appliqué, use long straight pins (glass heads are very good). Put only the tip into the fabric layers at the edge of your shape. This positions the shape neatly and enables you to pull out the pins easily as you sew.

• Another method of fixing the fabric appliqué to the background surface involves the use of Wonder-Under™ fabric adhesive. After you iron it onto the appliqué fabric, you peel away the paper and iron the shape to the background material, then satin-stitch it.

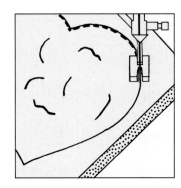

Baste the tracing of the shape to the underneath layer of fabric. Machine sew together, following the outline of the shape on the paper. When this is done, remove the paper.

The paper is transparent enough so it can be used for tracing shapes, or a template can be used to outline shapes on it. Make sure you reverse the pattern so the finished image will have the glue webbing on it.

• Using a new sharp needle in your sewing machine, sew a medium-length zigzag stitch around the very edge of the appliqué to secure it. Repeat using a satin stitch. When you start and finish sewing the shape, do not backstitch. Instead, leave the thread long enough so you can thread a needle and knot it on the underside for neater results.

Leaving a seam allowance, trim the shape outside the stitched line.

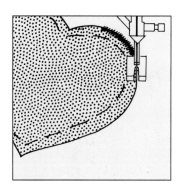

When satin stitching the appliqué on the machine, basting should be close to the edge, but should not interfere with the stitch.

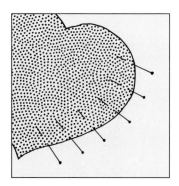

For pinning when machine sewing only, position the tip end of the pin into the appliqué. Leave a long end of the pin showing for easy removal as you sew.

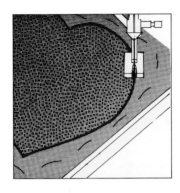

To start a faced appliqué, apply a traced drawing of the shape to two layers of fabric. Machine sew together, following the shape outline. Remove the paper and trim the shape, leaving a seam allowance.

Notch and cut appropriately. Make a slit in what will become the back of the appliqué. To complete, turn inside out and press with an iron.

Faced Appliqué

In faced appliqué, you use tracing paper patterns, as previously described in the section on templates.

• After tracing the shape, baste the paper to two layers of fabric you have chosen for the appliqué. Sew it on the machine following the outline of the drawing. Right sides of the fabric should be facing each other.

• Tear away the paper, and trim the shape. Notch appropriately (see page 95). Place the shape on your piece as it will appear when finished. Make a slit on the top side of this, and turn inside out. This will ensure the finished image (the side without the slit) will be right side up.

• Dampen the appliqué, and with a collar turner (a small bamboo device you can find in the notions department of your fabric store) turn out edges and press with an iron.

• The appliqué can be used as it is, or the facing side (the side with the slit) can be trimmed to the width of a seam allowance, eliminating the bulk of the second layer. This is determined by the weight of the fabric. If the fabric is thin, leave the facing side in to act as a liner, keeping the background from showing through.

This method gives you an accurate shape and finished edges that can now be easily hand- or machine-appliquéd.

Reverse Appliqué

In reverse appliqué you cut out a shape from the top surface to reveal one or more layers of fabric underneath. This allows you to use several layers at once, giving the work depth and intricacy. (See the fir tree in *Where the Heart Is . . . .*) Guatemalan molas (blouse panels) are worked in this way, and show how labyrinthine designs can get.

• Transfer the outline of shapes to the top fabric as you would with other appliqués.

• After the shape has been removed from the top surface, allowing 1/8 inch (3 mm) seam allowance, the outline of the shape with the edges tucked under is sewn to the second layer.

• The technique provides a method of obtaining accurate detail. It is easier to cut away the shape than to apply it to the surface.

A Mola (blouse panel) demonstrates extensive reverse appliqué.

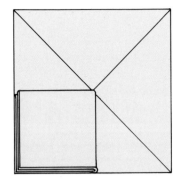

Fold the batting in quarters. Place at the center of the pressed X and unfold onto the backing.

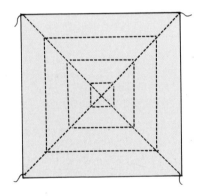

To baste layers of the quilt, first start in the middle and sew toward the corners. Then baste in concentric lines radiating from the center.

To this point, with the exception of the quilt-as-you-go methods, we have been preparing quilt tops. This section will give you the recipe for the textile sandwich as well as the quilting stitch and binding.   •   The quilt, by definition, is two outside layers held together by thread, to ensure the center substance, a padding, doesn't shift. This encompasses a broad variety of techniques and materials. It is not defined by size or ultimate use or purpose. Wall hangings, bed coverings, quilted clothing, and moving pads are all quilts.

The following instructions prepare the textile sandwich for hand-quilting in a hoop or frame as well as machine-quilting.

• The backing can be made by piecing two or three lengths of fabric and joining them to make the full size of your quilt. If you are using the self-binding method (see page 105) the backing should be about 3 inches (7.5 cm) larger on each side than the front. If the backing is made of a printed fabric, you won't have to worry about the appearance of your quilting on the underside.

• Iron the backing so it will lay flat. For guide marks, fold the quilt in half diagonally from corner to corner; iron it; fold again from the opposite corners to make a cross; and iron that. Thus creases created by the ironing are guide marks.

• Spread the backing on a large, even surface such as the floor, wrong side up, so it lays flat. Secure with masking tape at each corner as well as at intervals. Smooth out all ripples, but do not stretch the fabric.

• Fold the batting in quarters, and unfold it onto the backing, starting in the center of the pressed cross.

• Fold the quilt top in quarters, top side facing up, and unfold it onto the batting and backing, starting from the center as with batting. Pin the three layers together along the perimeter with safety pins. Pins are quicker than basting and should be set 4 to 5 inches (10-12.5 cm) apart.

• Whether you use pins or thread, start in the center of the top of the quilt, and work toward each corner, and start again in the center and out to each center side. Also baste concentric lines radiating from the center. You'll need about two hundred safety pins for a double-bed-sized quilt.

• If you are basting with thread, cut a long strand and thread your needle, taking one stitch in the center, using half the length of thread, leaving the other half as a long tail extending from the other side of first stitch. Finish sewing toward one corner. Thread your needle with the other half and continue in the opposite direction. This will prevent a lot of knots from accumulating in the center. You now have a textile sandwich.

SUPPORTING THE TEXTILE SANDWICH

Quilting in a hoop gives mobility to the quilter and is space efficient—two very relevant factors in present-day living. One drawback is that the finished quilt may not be as evenly flat or hang as well as if quilted in frame.

• Always start by placing the hoop in the center of the textile sandwich.

• Quilt this area (see *"The Quilting Stitch"* on page 103), and continue by moving the hoop in concentric circles out toward the edges. Do not leave your quilt in the hoop overnight. It will stretch and crease the fabric.

• When you reach the edge or corners, attach strips of fabric to the quilt, long and wide enough to allow you to quilt to the edges. Either sew or pin the strips with safety pins. Straight pins are apt to nick you.

Quilting in a frame is the best way of ensuring an evenly quilted, flat surface that hangs well. Frames also allow for more than one person to quilt at one time. They do take up a lot of space, however, usually the size of the quilt plus space around it. This is the main reason they are not used as often as hoops.

• If you are using a frame or quilting bars, you can do your basting, as well as your quilting, in the frame. The basting in a frame requires less tacking. Square the frame with a right angle. When rolling the textile sandwich onto the bars, try winding one side over and the other side under so that the shifting of the quilt top and the backing are equal.

• When the quilt is in an open frame, never leave the center area unsupported for any length of time or it will sag. To remedy this, place a card table or like support underneath.

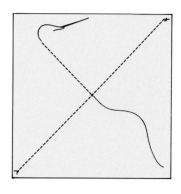

To avoid knots in center of the quilt, make sure you cut a length of thread sufficient to cover the area from corner to corner. Start sewing from the center, using half the length, then do the same using the other half of the thread.

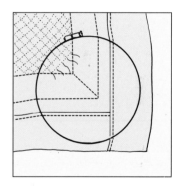

When using a hoop, attach strips to the quilt corners to enable you to finish the quilting.

THE HAND QUILTING STITCH

The quilting stitch is a series of running stitches that binds the three layers of the textile sandwich together. Ideally, the stitches are small and close together; but more important, the line should be fluid and the stitches evenly spaced. Start by taking one stitch at a time, and gradually try to pick up more than this. Let's say, three to four.

The degree of difficulty in quilting depends upon the type of fabric and the thickness of batting. In some areas of the quilt you may end up stab-stitching— putting the needle straight down through the layers completely and bringing it straight up again in a separate motion.

• Start with a length of thread, pull it through beeswax for smoother sewing, and wear a thimble on the second finger of your sewing hand. As a precaution, put a bandage on the second finger of your other hand.

• Bury the knot of the thread end by pulling it through the top to the batting.

• Pierce the top with the needle, using the thimbled finger to push and brushing the finger of your other hand underneath the quilt to ensure you have gone through the layers. Tilt the needle back up through the layers, using the thimble. Eventually, you will begin to use the needle in a rocking motion, picking up several stitches at a time. Don't lose heart, the quilting stitch will become a more rhythmic motion before long.

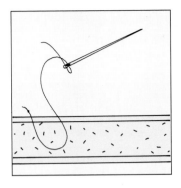

1. *Bury the knot of the thread end by pulling it through the top into the batting.*

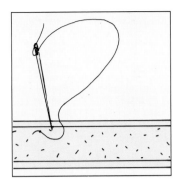

2. *Take one back stitch…*

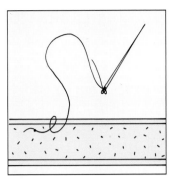

3. *Bring the needle up in front of the knot.*

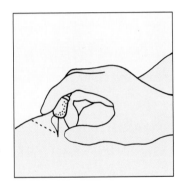

4. *Pierce the top with the needle.*

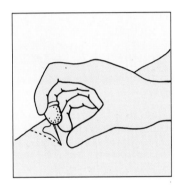

5. *Use the thimbled finger to push the needle.*

6. *Brush the finger of your other hand underneath the quilt.*

7. *Tilt the needle back up through the layers.*

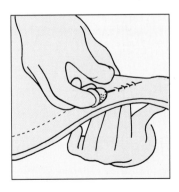

8. *Using the needle in a rocking motion, pick up several stitches at one time.*

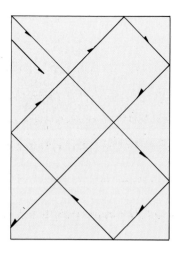

The quilt top is marked with a diagonal grid. Quilting starts in the upper left corner. By pivoting the needle to change direction, you can sew the quilt from side to side. Start again one line below the first in the upper left corner.

Machine-Quilting

Quilting by machine is always easier if the pieces are of manageable size, as in string quilting, but a whole quilt can be created this way.

• Before you start, make sure you have plenty of space around the machine and a support for the bulk of the work as you sew, behind your machine; thus the weight of the piece will not drag and cause problems while you are sewing. One solution is to sew on the dining room table.

• Use a presser foot that is open in front so you can see where you are sewing. Adjust your machine for a slightly longer stitch than usual as well as a bit looser tension. Do not backstitch the ends. Instead, pull them to the back of the work and thread them through a hand-sewing needle. Finish the stitching by taking several small stitches or knotting and lose the end of the thread between the layers. Then clip off the thread.

Diamond Grid Quilting: Machine Method 1

If you choose to do the quilting in a simple diagonal grid pattern, you can use the Ernest B. Haight machine-quilting method.

• The quilt top is marked with diagonal lines using a ruler and tailor's pencil, resulting in a diamond grid quilting pattern.

• The quilting starts in the upper-left-hand quarter and follows the diagonal line across the quilt. Keeping the needle positioned in the quilt, pivot following the right-angle line to the other side. And so on and sew on. Start again in the left-hand quarter, one line below the first. Continue in this manner until you have filled in all the lines.

Machine-Quilting: Method 2

If your quilt top cannot be quilted in as straightforward a manner as above, you should try this method:

• Roll up your textile sandwich from one side to the center. Flatten the roll and pin with safety pins, to prepare it for going under the arm of your machine.

• Roll up loosely the part that will be in your lap.

• Start your sewing in the central area, and move outward concentrically, rolling and unrolling the textile sandwich as you go. Try, if possible, to stitch moving away from completed areas, not toward them, as the fabric and batting will bunch up.

• For quilting around a shape, stop when the needle is still in the fabric. Lift the presser foot, pivot the quilt, lower the foot, and continue.

• As an extra precaution, while quilting a long, straight line, pin either side of that line to keep the fabric from puckering.

THE BINDING

The binding is the final touch that finishes the quilt. Choose the method of binding according to the design of the work and your personal preference.

Self-Binding

In the self-binding method, you've started at the beginning of the making of the textile sandwich with an outsize backing, 2 to 3 inches (5 to 7.5 cm) all around. This will become the binding of your quilt, so choose the backing material carefully.

• Trim any excess padding with scissors.

• Trim off the corners of the backing, approximately three-quarters of an inch (1.5 cm) from the corners of the quilt top. Fold the trimmed corner over the quilt top, and fold the sides in, with edges turned under to complete the mitered corner.

• Fold the excess backing material over to the front, turning under the raw edges, and secure with straight pins. Baste and remove pins.

• Hand- or machine-sew down edges.

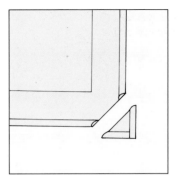

Trim off the corners of the backing.

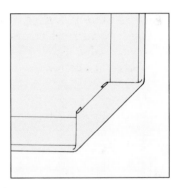

Fold in the edges and the corner.

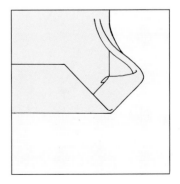

Complete the mitered corner.

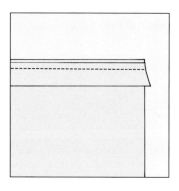

1. Strips are sewn to opposite sides.

2. Strips are folded over with edges turned under.

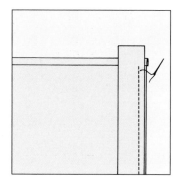

3. Remaining strips a little longer than the quilt are added to the other sides.

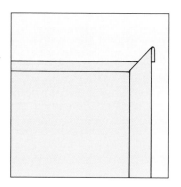

4. Each corner is either folded over or mitered.

Strip-Binding

Strip-binding uses four separate bands of material wide enough to wrap around the perimeter edge of the quilt; each strip is long enough to cover one side adequately.

• Cut straight strips for the four sides.

• Sew strips to two opposite sides—folded over, edges turned under, and pinned and finished on the machine or hand hemmed, according to your preference.

• Add the remaining strips to the other sides of the quilt. They should extend a little past each corner to be either folded over or mitered for finishing the corners.

Continuous Strip-Binding

This type of binding consists of strips joined together to form one continuous band long enough to go around the perimeter of the quilt.

• Cut strips, ends joined on a diagonal, as in store-bought biased binding. Strips need not be cut on a bias unless you are finishing a quilt with a scalloped edge or curved corners.

• When you have joined enough strips to go around the quilt, starting at some mid-point along one side of the quilt, pin and sew, until you complete the perimeter.

• Turn edges under, and fold over. Pin. Baste and remove pins. Hand- or machine-sew, mitering the corners.

Having finished your quilt, sign and date it.

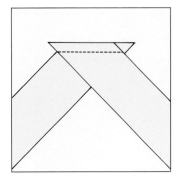

1. Cut strips, ends joined on a diagonal.

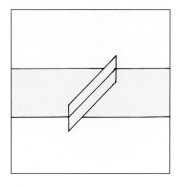

2. Joined ends.

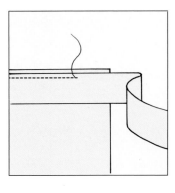

3. Starting mid-point, pin and sew.

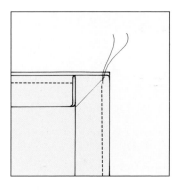

4. Sew around entire perimeter.

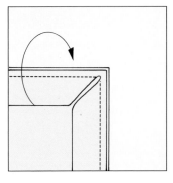

5. Turn edges under and fold over.

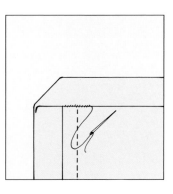

6. Finish by sewing and mitering corners.

CHAPTER FIVE

*Designing For the
Child in You*

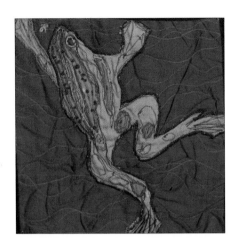

Each block in this quilt, made for
Charlotte Sohr by Deborah Kaplan
and friends, provides a window into a
child's world.

I have a theory that our love of fabric and quilts stems from childhood experiences. These experiences are associated with touch, comfort, and security. I remember a very pretty, striped, soft-woven blanket; snowy white pillows edged in fancy filigree; and dresses made of red Swiss-dot organza, sea-blue taffeta, and sweet white light cotton. I also remember an aunt who had all of my cousin's outgrown dresses made into a braided rug she put by her bed.

Needlework and sewing fascinated me as a child. I remember learning bits of embroidery, knitting, and crochet. I started using a sewing machine when I was ten and sewed all the time. It helped that my mother owned a fabric shop. When I got older I made a quilt. It was made of simple star blocks, the material for each shape carefully composed by trading colors and patterns of fabric with friends.

This quilt combined all the elements I found attractive in needlework. Appreciating the tactility and visual richness of the materials stimulated my youthful creative energy. This was my first quilt. I was sixteen years old.

With the exception of four years of art school, I have been assembling and quilting fabric ever since. This is not an uncommon history of events among quilt and fabric enthusiasts. Interest in fabric construction begins most often in some childhood experience. Young adulthood takes us in other directions, creative or otherwise. Later, mature and more patient, we return to the quilting medium. The quilt and the quilter are both part of a cycle.

Whether themes are inspired by memories or fantasies of childhood or even a child's view of the world, called forth by one's own offspring, it is interesting to note the natural affinity between the topic and the medium. This does not always mean childlike, although it can be child related or even allegorical, using imaginary characters portrayed and given life in fabric and quilting.

I wish fabric work would be used more often as illustrative material for children's stories. For instance, the piece *Ugly Duckling*, which is shown on page 45 in Chapter Two was inspired by Hans Christian Andersen's famous story. His stories, in their original Danish version, were allegorical fables for adults as well as children. I tried to convey that knowledge through portraying the rude ducks as being all the same, while the figure they were making fun of was, of course, a swan, who in time would be much more beautiful than those tormenting her.

Sylvia Price's **Lillian** *combines traditional block patterns with images of cats made of geometric shapes.*

L'alla Rookh, by Carol Goddu, is inspired by the stories of *A Thousand and One Nights,* or *Arabian Nights.* The legend has it that these stories were told by Scheherazade, to keep her husband, the wicked Sultan, from killing her, as he had all his other wives. These very adult fantasies have been kept alive for centuries as both adult and children's stories. They are the source of "Ali Baba and the Forty Thieves," "Aladdin and His Magic Lamp," and others and have inspired countless movies, books, and works of art.

In this quilted work by Goddu, the fabrics used were once only found in the exotic East, where these stories originated. The desire for these fabrics was one of the main reasons for Marco Polo's journeys, which opened relations between East and West. Fabric, history, and fantasy are richly interlaced in this wonderful work, in ways that can be relished by children and grown-ups alike.

Dreams, by Suesi Metcalf, is a visual treasure of Victorian childhood. It evokes this era in both its subject and use of fabrics. On the front, a beautiful, soft, silken child lays his head on a pillow trimmed in filigree and covered in a pattern of "baby blocks" made of the sumptuous fabrics so lovingly used in that time. Somehow the reality of that world seems so remote in our time of efficient and practical thinking. It is a lovely world, however, in which to indulge the imagination. Metcalf takes us one step further into this fantasy by placing elaborate Victorian dolls in the back of the quilt. *Dreams* is a fully realized work of art.

In *Lillian,* Sylvia Price employs a device that children give to their drawings to make certain items more important—that is, making the main character larger. Lillian is Sylvia's cat, and she is watching through the window as a parade of neighborhood cats go by her food bowl, finishing off what was left in it.

Left: **L'alla Rookh,** *by Carol Goddu, was inspired by the Arabian Nights.*
Below: **Dreams,** *by Suesi Metcalf, shows a child sleeping under the pattern of "baby blocks", a quilt within a quilt.*

Animal Parade, *by Roz Haines portrays order and calm.*

The piecing of the figures integrated with the pieced background make it an intriguing puzzle, not unlike the sheep in *Morning Graze,* by Flavin Glover, on page 24 in Chapter One, made up of log cabin blocks. Animals always seem to have child appeal and reveal the softer side of human nature. Therefore the combination of our feelings and fabric are very naturally interpreted with animal themes.

Roz Haines does this with Animal Parade. These lovely pastel renderings of different

animals repeated across the quilt communicate a feeling of harmony and peace. This work conveys calm to both the adult and child viewer.

In *Jungle Friends*, by Ann Bird, I feel as if I've come across a page in a children's story book. I would like to eavesdrop on the conversation between Elephant and Giraffe, two bigger-than-life creatures inhabiting a faraway land. The subjects and the fabrics they are made of are playful. The eye travels from object to object in a circular motion. The absence of figures in the middle of the picture gives it a unique feeling of expectation. What will happen next? Bird made this piece for a child, and a major factor in its success is the strength of its simplicity. It does not give away the whole story.

Most quilted work leans toward interpreting more feminine themes, and naturally so, since the medium originated in women's hands. There is a balance in nature, though, thank goodness, and it crosses over into quilting. Many men like quilts as much as women, but often for different reasons. Men don't usually look at quilts and say, "Wow, look at that fine stitching!" or "What great use of fabric!" Their response is more directly connected with the emotional impact of the visual. It is pure and unaffected.

Several men have contributed to this book, and since I made my choices of what quilts to include by viewing the works first and then finding out the stories behind them, I can honestly say each work was chosen for its visual impact. In all cases each work had to sing its own unique and special song to be included. There were some hard choices, but whether the artist was male or female never entered into the equation.

Creepy Crawlies—Misunderstood Marvels, *by Anne Morrell.*

Creepy Crawlies, by Anne Morrell, deals humorously with an unusual theme. I remember as a child being interested in things that crawled and wiggled. I am sure this quilter had that same appreciation, which inspired her to create this design. My own four-year-old boy, Jacob, recently went through a stage in which he brought me Sam the Praying Mantis, Ugh the Bug, and a dead mouse he found outside that he said had "only fainted." These subjects have not as yet inspired me, but they do give insight into this child's psyche and interests. It remains to be seen whether he quilts in the future.

He recently showed new interest, however, in his baby quilt, which my stepdaughters and I made for him before he was born, and that did give me an idea. I found him one day running his cars around the outer strips of its log cabin pattern. Not long after this, Jake led me down the aisle of the local drugstore to an unanticipated toy section, and my attention was directed to a folded plastic sheet, packaged in a clear plastic bag.

Jake explained to me that this was "a great toy" that he could "play cars on." It was a fold-out roadway with different prominent town buildings—firehouse, hotel, railway station, garage, grocery store, and the like—printed on it. I got the picture. Yes, lots of play value here, although I didn't particularly care for the look of it.

I bought it anyway. Later on that evening he asked me to spread it over his bed so he could play with his cars before going to sleep. And there it was: Jake's quilt—a modern-day version of Robert Louis Stevenson's poem *A Pleasant Land of Counterpane.* It will have hills and valleys and fields and lakes and towns and countryside and lots of roads with lots of places to stop. It will be based on the topography of our own geographical area, a three-hundred-year-old small city on one of the Great Lakes. It will, I hope, be on his bed for next Christmas.

This chapter on the child in us closes with Lois Epp's patchwork quilt *Deux Images: Four Seasons.* For me, this quilt represents the wonderful patchwork quilts in children's story books. Not only does it have brilliant and varied colors, there is plenty of playful diversity in the geometric shapes as well as in the specific imagery, such as tulips and maple leaves. This quilt will take a child through many seasons, and I can well imagine one discovering many delights while lying under its cover.

Deux Images: Four Seasons, *by Lois Epp is a colorful patchwork with a difference.*

CHAPTER SIX

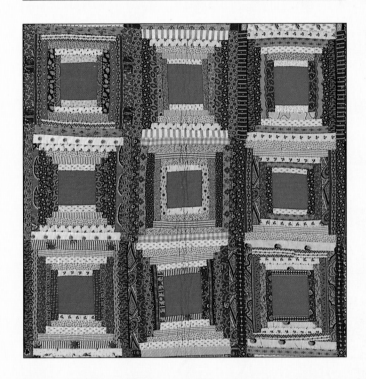

Grand Finale — Long Live Quilts

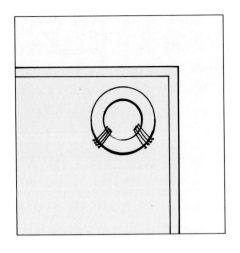

Sew a washer at these two places.

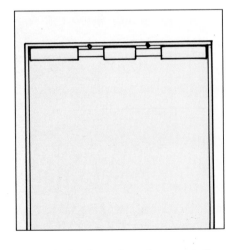

Break the sleeve into three parts for even hanging of the quilt.

The methods for hanging work are most often determined by the size of the quilt and where it is placed. For larger works, I prefer a wooden bar and Velcro™ for permanent installations. An insert sleeve and dowel or flat bar, however, is more versatile for exhibition purposes or temporary situations. For smaller pieces, I suggest metal washers from the hardware store because they are discreet in size and do the job adequately.

METAL WASHERS

For small wall hangings and freestyle shapes—such as circles, stars, and the like—one of the simplest methods is to add a metal washer about 1 inch (2.5 cm) in from each top corner or point. Attach the washers by sewing in two places.

POLE OR FLAT BAR

Add a sleeve to the top of the back of the quilted work. The sleeve should be made up of three separate strips, to provide open areas. Two screw eyes are attached to a pole, also called a *dowel*, or a flat wooden bar or slat of correct length, a little shorter than the quilt width. The screw eyes will appear in the open areas when the pole or slat is inserted in the sleeve. The quilt will hang evenly supported when the screw eyes are attached to cords or suspended from L hooks.

The hardware and the pole or slat are readily available from lumber-supply stores. Ask for a cured wood that won't warp with time. After lightly sanding the pole or slat, coat with clear acrylic to prevent any seepage of acid or other chemicals present in the wood.

VELCRO™ AND FLAT BAR

Measure the width of the quilt and cut a strip of the two sides of the Velcro™ accordingly. Machine-sew the hook side of the Velcro™ to a cloth tape of the same length and a slightly greater width than the Velcro™. Hand-sew this to the top of the back of the quilt. Glue the furry side of the Velcro™ strip to a nonwarping

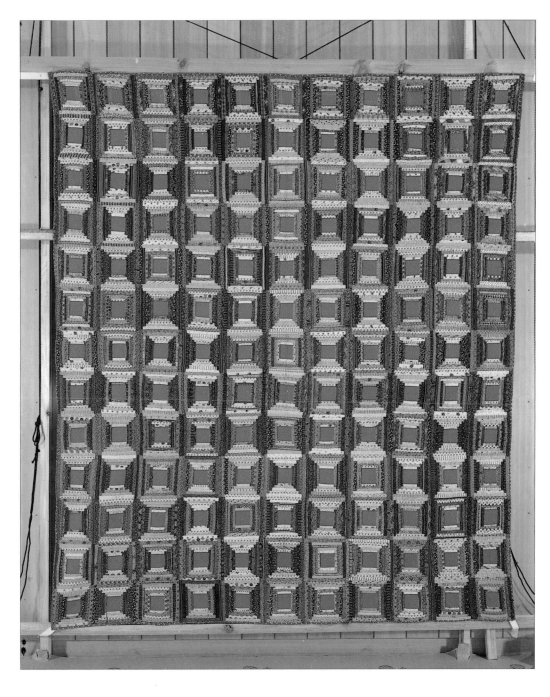

One example of a hanging quilt. Courthouse steps pattern from The Shelburne Museum.

wooden bar treated with acrylic, as above. Reinforce the Velcro™ to the bar by stapling, with a staple gun, at about 4-inch (10-cm) intervals. Affix the slat to the wall, and attach the quilt to it. This method allows you to remove the quilt easily from the wall for its periodic cleaning.

It is easier to preserve than restore. Here are some tips to prevent us from inadvertently destroying our work and for prolonging the life of the quilt.

ENVIRONMENTAL FACTORS

Strong, direct sunlight will not only fade fabrics but destroy them. Any constant light, especially fluorescent or even an incandescent lamp, will do injury over a period of time, hardly noticeable until the damage is done.

Flourescent tubes can be covered with special, clear Mylar™ jackets, which filter out the harmful ultraviolet rays. This is especially necessary if the work is on permanent display in a building illuminated with flourescent lighting.

If you are using an incandescent spotlight to light your quilt in a dark area, the bulb should not be close enough to the piece to create a hot spot. It is recommended that the light should be 10 feet (3 m) away from the piece and its position moved periodically, so it is not hitting the same spot all the time.

There are special bulbs for just this consideration, called neo-white incandescent. With these bulbs, yellow light is filtered out and less heat is given off. For availability, see the appendix.

Windows, as well as having drapes and blinds drawn through the brightest part of the day, can be coated with a special plastic sheet that filters out the ultraviolet rays. This plastic comes in clear or slightly tinted sheets that can be applied directly to the glass. They are also energy savers. See the appendix for sources of these products.

Humidity and climate are also factors in the preservation of quilts. Generally, quilts like the same temperature and amount of humidity that people do. There should not be a lot of fluctuation of either. Good air circulation and fifty percent humidity comprise the best balance of factors.

CLEANING

Avoid washing your quilts as much as possible if you don't want to wear them out. Periodically, about every four to six months, place them face down on a sheet, and vacuum them from the back. This should be done gently as possible with the drapery attachment or a small hand vacuum. Turn the quilt over, place a bed sheet or nylon window screen on the quilt top, and gently vacuum through it.

When it does come time to wash your quilt, if you have pre-washed your fabrics, you shouldn't have to worry about shrinkage. You might, however, want to test areas, especially red fabric, for bleeding. Dampen the test area and dab with blotting paper. If it does bleed, consider dry cleaning. Your local museum's textile department can recommend a dry cleaner who will take proper care.

If you are washing, choose a warm summer day, so that you can dry the quilt outside. Begin by folding your quilt accordion style, and immerse it in warm, mild, soapy water in the bathtub. Press down gently with the flat of your hands to remove the dirt. Turn and refold in the tub as best you can, and proceed with this gentle washing method.

Drain the tub, pressing out the water with the flat of your hands. Refill with water for the rinse. Repeat until the rinse water is clear of soap. Leave the quilt in the tub for a while to drain further. Upon return, try to press out more moisture by pressing gently with towels.

When you think you can remove the quilt without too much strain on you or it, fold it lengthwise into thirds, carry it outside to a shaded area, and lay it face down on a sheet to dry. Lay down a top sheet as well, to protect it from bird droppings and other debris.

STORAGE

The quilt, when not in use, should be loosely rolled with a covering of acid-free tissue paper and placed in a drawer or box. Periodically it should be taken out and rerolled.

For neowhite incandescent bulbs
and daylight-balanced fluorescent tubes:

CANADA

Duro-test Electric Ltd.

419 Attwell Drive

Rexdale, ONT M9W 5W5

(416) 675-1623

U.K.

Osram Ltd.

P.O. Box 17

East Lane

Wembley

Middlesex

HA9 7PG

081-904 4321

U.K.

CLE Design Ltd

Industrial Lighting Designers

69 Haydons Road

London

SW19 1HQ

081-540 5772

CANADA

Convenience Products

44 Advance Road

Toronto, ONT M8Z 2T4

(416) 239-3523

BIBLIOGRAPHY

Edwards, Betty, *Drawing on the Right Side of the Brain.* J.P. Tarcher Inc.: 1979.

Fanning, Robbie and Tony, *The Complete Book of Machine Quilting.* Chilton Book Company: 1980.

James, Michael, *The Quiltmaker's Handbook.* Prentice-Hall: 1978.

Loyd, Sam, *The Eighth Book of Tan.* Dover: 1968.

Stothers, Marilyn, *Curved Strip-Piecing, A New Technique.* PH Press: 1988.

Swim, Laurie, *The Joy of Quilting.* Viking Canada: 1984. The Main Street Press: 1986.

Walker, Michele, *The Complete Book of Quiltmaking.* Knopf, U.S., Frances Lincoln, U.K.: 1986.

INDEX

W

PICTURE CREDITS AND ACKNOWLEDGMENTS

Front jacket photograph courtesy of
   Anne de la Mauviniere Silva

Back jacket photograph © Nir Bareket

PRINCIPAL PHOTOGRAPHY BY:

NIR BAREKET, Toronto, pp. 32b, 33a, 44a,
   44b, 45b, 46a, 50, 52a, 52b, 53a, 53b, 63,
   66b, 69b, 71b, 73, 74a, 74b, 74c, 75a, 75b,
   75c, 75d, 75e

JOHN GRUEN, New York, pp. 18b, 19a,
   26b, 29, 34, 51, 61, 99a, 99b, 110a, 110b

JEREMY JONES, Toronto, pp. 17, 20b, 21a,
   40, 56, 58a, 58b, 109, 113a, 117a, 117b

With other contributions from:

Ann Bird, pp. 19b, 21b, 44c, 45a, 115

Bridgeman/Art Resource, New York, p. 10

Sheila Brokloff, p. 22

Barbara Carlson, pp. 70a, 70b

Erika Carter, p. 20a

John Dean, Calgary, p. 35

Jean Evans, p. 59

Jackie Gilmore, p. 69a

Flavin Glover, pp. 24a, 24b

Larry Goldstein, p. 71a

Roslyn Hanes, p. 114

Douglas Henderson, Ontario, pp. 54a,
   54b, 54c

Alan Isaksen, p. 99a

Vicki L. Johnson, p. 33

Deborah Kaplan, pp. 99b, 110a, 110b

Angelika Kraus-Werth, pp. 55a, 55b

The Maritime Life Assurance Company,
   Halifax, Nova Scotia, p. 60

Ernest Mayer, Winnipeg, pp. 23a, 23b

John Melville, Vancouver, pp. 39, 57, 64

Suesi Metcalf, p. 113b

Joyce Murrin, p. 59

Museum of American Folk Art, p. 24c

Miriam Nathan-Roberts, p. 85b

Sylvia G. Price, pp. 37b, 112

Shelburne Museum, Shelburne,
   Vermont, pp. 77, 85a, 90g

Anne de la Mauviniere Silva, pp. 8, 25a,
   36a, 36b

Laurie Sobie, p. 19c

Judith Tinkl, p. 37a

Doris Waddell, p. 112

P.J. Wall, Dartmouth, Nova Scotia, p. 116